TEACHING
DESIGN

**A Guide to Curriculum and Pedagogy
for College Design Faculty and Teachers
Who Use Design in Their Classrooms**

Meredith Davis

ALLWORTH
PRESS

Allworth Press books may be purchased in bulk at special discounts for sales promotion, corporate gifts, fund-raising, or educational purposes. Special editions can also be created to specifications. For details, contact the Special Sales Department, Allworth Press, 307 West 36th Street, 11th Floor, New York, NY 10018 or info@skyhorsepublishing.com.

20 19 18 17 16   5 4 3 2 1

Published by Allworth Press, an imprint of Skyhorse Publishing, Inc. 307 West 36th Street, 11th Floor, New York, NY 10018.

Allworth Press® is a registered trademark of Skyhorse Publishing, Inc.®, a Delaware corporation.

www.allworth.com

Cover design by Meredith Davis
Cover photo credit Matthew Peterson

Library of Congress Cataloging-in-Publication Data is available on file.

Print ISBN: 978-1-62153-530-0
Ebook ISBN: 978-1-62153-531-7

Printed in the United States of America

CONTENTS

FOREWORD

I t is surprising that there are so few books on teaching design, given the expanding size of the educational workforce in the field, very little college coursework on teaching design, and growing interest by K-12 teachers and university faculty from outside design in a design-thinking pedagogy. For the most part, architecture and design faculty have neither pre-service nor in-service training for their role as teachers. They arrive in academic positions from graduate programs in design and professional practice, not from the study of curriculum and pedagogy more typical of teachers in K-12 schools. As an art education major at Pennsylvania State University in the 1960s before later study in design, I was required to take courses in the psychology of learning, philosophies of education, and sociology of teaching. I spent a full semester in high school teaching under the mentorship of an established educator and in supporting night classes required by the university to make sense of my full-time classroom experiences. While my college education couldn't prepare me for the unpredictable realities of managing a classroom, it did provide me with a "meta" view of teaching that guides my work in and with complex institutions today.

Even more puzzling is limited recognition by design professionals regarding the contribution of education to practitioners' worldviews of the discipline. Some designers question whether formal education in design is necessary, arguing that novices can acquire skills on the job or through self-education. Others debate the possible outcomes of two-year versus four-year programs or the relevance of qualifications in graduates of master's programs. And while there is general acknowledgment that particular institutions produce certain kinds of design professionals, there is little analysis regarding exactly how these curricula and pedagogies impart specific values toward an evolving context for the field. With the exception of the Bauhaus, not much of recent design history is attributed specifically to the proselytizing effects of training and education.

At the same time, K–12 educators and college faculty in other domains who want to use a design-based approach to teaching and learning in any discipline cite a lack of literature in support of their interests. A study by the National Endowment for the Arts found that K–12 teachers who used design strategies in their classrooms generally had no background in design and learned about it through loose associations with design practitioners. They often felt adrift in the absence of appropriate references for their professional development. Similarly, college faculty seeking ways to increase students' critical and creative thinking find few resources that describe practical strategies for applying design pedagogy to other college disciplines.

The purpose of this book, therefore, is to provide discussions of teaching and learning that fill gaps in the preparation of the professoriate. It is also to offer suggestions regarding practices for developing, articulating, and assessing curricula in an academic climate of increasing accountability and competition for resources.

In one sense, this book is ideologically agnostic toward the literal subject matter of education. There is no attempt to endorse a particular view of design that serves all programs or disciplines well. At the same time, discussions also reflect a fervent belief that curricular structure and pedagogy influence students' lifetime goals and perspectives on the consequences of their work. How faculty organize what they teach and the methods through which they deliver content reflect a particular worldview against which designers evaluate professional responsibilities. In this sense, the book encourages rethinking design education for the rapidly changing context in which today's students will spend their careers.

PART I
TEACHING *ABOUT* DESIGN

Unlike many professions in which practitioners study for their life's work through specialized training, college and university faculty rarely prepare for their roles as teachers. They master disciplinary knowledge through focused undergraduate and graduate study, but few undergo instruction for imparting expertise to novices. Some faculty come to the teaching profession naturally, with strong skills for interacting with beginners, speaking publicly, and inventing learning experiences. Others mature as teachers on the job, while the consequences of their early struggles affect generations of students who enroll in their classes.

Complicating faculty lives is increasing pressure on college-level design programs to conform to the values and behaviors of institutions that look more and more like businesses. It is no longer possible to ignore a counting and measuring culture that allocates resources on the basis of competitive proposals, assesses effectiveness using standardized metrics, incentivizes particular kinds of scholarship, and rewards programs and faculty for their ability to achieve national reputations. Maintaining the authenticity of design curricula and instruction under the weight of these mandates requires that faculty and program administrators frame teaching and learning in ways that are also accountable to the strategic environment in which their programs exist.

At the same time, architecture and design are rapidly changing fields. Standing still is not an option; neither is simply reacting to the immediate hiring practices of local design offices whose interests are in the short-term skills of entry-level designers. Today's design programs must prepare students for evolving with the field across fifty-year professional careers, responding to shifting paradigms for practice, and solving problems that are new to their fields. More importantly, colleges and universities prepare productive citizens who shape the world we live in through the type of inquiry a design education instills. This is not a responsibility faculty can leave to chance or view only as student preparation for employment.

The purpose of *Part I: Teaching about Design*, therefore, is to redress in some small way the missing education of college design faculty. In the opening chapter, the book traces the history of design education as evidence that many of the long-standing teaching traditions arose from very specific conditions. The chapter on curriculum development provides practical strategies for building programs that respond both to a counting-and-measuring culture and a changing profession. A chapter on what makes a good design project helps design practitioners distinguish between client-based work in design offices and learning experiences for students. The current emphasis on interdisciplinary engagement inspired the chapter on teaching collaboration and the implications of general education in design. The last chapter in Part I addresses assessment at the levels of student work and curriculum effectiveness, with concrete discussions of standards and rubrics.

CHAPTER I:
A BRIEF HISTORY OF DESIGN EDUCATION

FROM TRADES TO PROFESSIONS

Today's design fields began as *trades*, rather than *professions*. Artisans produced graphic communication, crafted objects of practical use, fashioned the interiors of buildings, and constructed shelter. Focused on the practical work of making things, new practitioners acquired expertise through on-the-job training. As early as the twelfth century, apprenticeship systems in Europe prepared people for work in design trades: traces of this approach to design education can still be found in some practices today.

In contrast to trades, modern professions have documented histories, bodies of literature that contain the accumulated knowledge of the discipline and practice, codes of ethics and standards of fair practice, critical discourse, efforts devoted exclusively to the generation of new knowledge, and formal strategies and institutions for educating new professionals. The professions of graphic, industrial, and interior design have origins in the twentieth century, especially in the United States.

The American Institute of Graphic Arts formed in 1914 as a small club of illustrators, graphic artists, printers, and publishers in New York (Heller & Gluck, 1989). The organization's website describes the original forty members as "the old guard for a new profession" (Heller & Gluck, 1989). Design historian Steven Heller characterized their motives as an attempt to preserve the high art of typography and printing, threatened by the visual clutter of nineteenth-century ephemera and new, cheaper printing technologies (Heller & Gluck, 1989). The founders' constitution reflected their professional and educational purposes:

To stimulate and encourage those engaged in the graphic arts; to form
a center for intercourse and the exchange of views of all interested
in these arts; to publish books and periodicals, to hold exhibitions in
the United States and participate as far as possible in the exhibitions
held in foreign countries relating to graphic arts; to invite exhibitions of foreign works; to stimulate public taste by school exhibitions,
lectures, and printed matter; promote the higher education in these
arts, and generally do all things which will raise the standard and aid
the extension and development of graphic arts in the United States
(Heller & Gluck, 1989).

William Leiss attributed the development of the industrial design profession
in the United States to the rise of advertising in the first half of the twentieth
century. Although nineteenth-century American products had a strong reputation for engineering and durability, their appearance suffered when compared to their European counterparts (Leiss, 1990). The Industrial Designers
Society of America (IDSA) traces public recognition of industrial design
in the United States to a 1927 "Exposition of Art in Trade" organized by
Macy's Department Store, which featured "modern products" from a 1925
International Exposition of Modern Decorative and Industrial Arts in Paris
(Gantz, 2015). Advertisers encouraged American manufacturers to change
the surface qualities of their goods to compete with European imports. They
surrounded products with attractive advertising images of a prosperous modern life, promoting public consumption through desire for the next new
style and purchase of *ensembles* of coordinated products that shared formal
characteristics.

The first recorded interior decoration commission in the United States
was to Elsie de Wolfe, who went on to write a 1913 book titled *The House
in Good Taste* (IDLNY, 2016). The field grew through the efforts of furniture companies, which expanded their services to include advice about
textiles, wall treatments, and architectural features that complemented their
products. Dorothy Draper—the first documented designer of commercial
interiors—established her firm in 1923 (IDLNY, 2016). She was known for
colorful interiors in otherwise drab business environments and the design
of luxury hotels in a number of American cities. The term "interior design"
was coined in the 1930s by a magazine titled *Interior Design and Decoration* (IDLNY, 2016). A year later, the American Institute of Decorators was

established, eventually merging with other organizations and changing its name to the American Society of Interior Designers (ASID). Originally associated with the work of homemakers, not professionals, the study of interior design began in home economics programs. It was not until 1982 that the first title registration legislation supported professional status for interior design practice (IDLNY, 2016).

Architecture has a slightly longer professional history than other design fields in the United States. The American Institute of Architects formed in 1857 with the intent "to promote the artistic, scientific, and practical profession to its members; to facilitate their intercourse and good fellowship; to elevate the standing of the profession; and to combine the efforts of those engaged in the practice of Architecture, for the general advancement of the Art" (AIA, 2016). In 1867, the AIA debated establishing a national school of architecture based on the École des Beaux-Arts in Paris for teaching evening classes in drawing, aesthetics, and the history of art and architecture (AIA, 2016). Instead, the membership chose to support an existing program at Massachusetts Institute of Technology, which was followed later by new programs at the University of Illinois and Cornell, Columbia, and Tuskegee Universities. No legal definition of what it meant to be an "architect" appeared before 1897 when Illinois adopted a licensing law, but it was another fifty years before all states had established standards for architectural licensure (AIA, 2016).

The history of design practice, therefore, is one of transition from trades to professions; from purely instrumental know-how gained through employment to academic preparation that includes study of the discipline as well as the practice—that is, the theories, perspectives, and discourse that underpin professional decision-making. Increasing demand for professional design services in the United States during the twentieth century raised the importance of college-level programs in ensuring a predictable supply of competent designers. However, the curricular and pedagogical practices of American programs owed much to educational systems in Europe, dating from medieval guilds through the immigration of design teachers to the United States during World War II. The following discussions trace important influences on contemporary design education. While the list of examples is far from complete, the purpose in describing them is to identify educational practices and philosophies that shaped much of today's study in design.

EUROPEAN CRAFT GUILDS AND APPRENTICESHIP SYSTEMS

Economic historian Stephan Epstein described the craft guild as "a formal association of artisans that functioned both as buyers of raw materials and as sellers of finished goods" (Epstein, 1998, p. 685). The eleventh and twelfth centuries saw development of a strong merchant class engaged in trade and commerce that supported growing populations in European cities, a consumer society whose citizens no longer produced everything they needed through privately owned land and labor. Although merchants imported commodities from afar, there was a need to convert raw materials, such as wool and metals, into objects of practical use. Out of this need emerged craft guilds that regulated the production of goods, product quality, apprentice training, and guild members' conduct. The guild controlled the practice of their craft in a particular town or region and depended on letters of patent from a local ruling authority to enforce trade and to retain ownership of tools and materials. By the fourteenth century, there were more than one hundred craft guilds in cities throughout Europe (Weisner-Hanks et al., 2003). These guilds dominated craft production well into the sixteenth century.

Epstein argued that the real benefits of the guilds—that is, advantages that could not have been achieved through other means—were the reduced costs of training a skilled workforce and making efficient use of labor without the risk of losing trade secrets (Epstein, 1998). Guild masters offset the expense of educating novices through entry fees charged to apprentices and discouraged default on their obligations or jumping to another master by starting wages below market levels and raising them across time with the promise of a payoff at the end of service (Epstein, 1998). Masters also held the rights to work produced by apprentices, a practice that may account for attitudes by today's colleges and universities regarding the ownership and use of student work. In return, guilds enforced adequate training of their members and guaranteed proficiency and employment for at least one economic cycle (Epstein, 1998).

Apprentices spent a designated number of years learning their craft, eventually advancing to journeyman status by working in the shop of a master. After completing service as journeymen, they crafted *masterpieces* through which master craftsmen judged their worthiness for acceptance as full members of the guild. Although the amount of time spent at each level of training varied from craft to craft and from town to town, all craftsmen went through this three-stage process before opening a shop as a master.

Most guilds restricted membership to males: young, unmarried men typically lived with the master's family during their years as apprentices and journeymen before earning full guild membership. In this way, the guilds represented a process of socialization for young men by establishing peer groups engaged in the same training (Weisner-Hanks et al., 2003). During economic downturns, the guilds limited the number of full members. Some men remained at the journeyman level for their entire lives or broke with their masters to form journeymen's guilds that protested the working regulations of the master guild (Weisner-Hanks et al., 2003).

The formation of a guild required town approval and, once sanctioned, held a monopoly over particular kinds of work. Competition among masters was controlled by the amount of raw material each master could own and the size of his workshop (Weisner-Hanks et al., 2003). Limits on guild size and the number of hours apprentices and journeymen could work discouraged experimentation with new processes that required more workers or that lowered the cost of finished goods (Weisner-Hanks et al., 2003). Although there is debate among scholars on this point, it is generally accepted that guilds were not hotbeds of innovation. Even when they experimented with new techniques, they tended to retreat back into traditional practices best suited to their scale and limited resources. Epstein cites journeyman migration as a primary means for technological innovation. As restless craftsmen relocated, often across regional boundaries, they took ways of doing things with them (Epstein, 1998).

Many guilds prohibited the use of machinery, guaranteeing the special status of handicraft expertise gained through training and the role of the master craftsman in setting standards. Larger production operations took place outside the city where the guilds had no regulatory powers. They were called *cottage industries*, a reference to the frequent employment of entire households in a single production activity. Because cottage industries had lower costs than city guilds, they attracted investors who did none of the work but provided raw materials. This alternate system of production threatened the guild system. A first-stage form of capitalism, cottage industries marked an early division of labor that led to eighteenth-century factories in which work was done outside the home and workers were paid as individuals (Weisner-Hanks et al., 2003).

In the 1700s, the French worried that guild apprenticeships were not serving the needs of children and hindered French economic development. They developed drawing schools to fill the gap between children's completion of public school at age twelve and entry to apprenticeships around age fifteen. In 1746, Ferrand de Monthelon published the *Project for the Establishment of Free Drawing Schools*, expressing concern over children's idleness before entering an apprenticeship and declaring that drawing was fundamental pretraining for most trades (Crowston, 2009). A number of prominent French craftsmen concurred that drawing schools allowed students to determine their aptitudes without the seemingly endless time spent as apprentices and journeymen. Jean-Jacques Bachelier—former artistic director for the manufacture of royal porcelain—established the first free drawing school in Paris in 1766. The École Royale Gratuite de Dessin enrolled 1,500 male students in a six-year curriculum that included four hours of study a week in "architecture and geometry, the human figure and animals, and flowers and ornamentation" (Crowston, 2009, p. 58). Originally intended as pre-apprentice training, the school eventually served as continuing education for students already engaged in apprenticeships (Crowston, 2009).

The craft guilds established the first organized system of design education and had lasting impact on design practices, how designers prepare for professional work, and definitions of craft. The apprentice system of the guilds shaped later educational models and defined hiring practices in design offices well into the twentieth century. For much of the late twentieth century in communication design, for example, recent graduates of college-level programs started their design careers as production artists in the preparation of a senior designer's work for printing. They gained control of project direction and form only after mastering the technical aspects of the print production process. The introduction of computer-assisted design in the mid-1980s toppled that hierarchy in many design offices. Software quickly collapsed the processes of form generation and technical production and the newest employees were often the most experienced in digital work. New practices, such as design strategy and interaction design, emerged to fill the gap left by technological advancements. These practices diversified the skill sets sought by employers and, in some cases, the missions of various design schools. Today, there are distinct areas of communication design practice, and the management of technology is too specialized to serve as a first step to a design career. Instead, most students enter laterally, rather than vertically through production, into different areas of practice.

The contemporary design internship, however, continues the traditions of the apprentice system for students in college or immediately after graduation.

In the field of architecture, for example, preparation for taking the licensure examination requires 3,640 hours of Internship Development experience in a professional office across four content categories: predesign, design, project management, and practice management.

Internships have recently come under scrutiny by the judicial system and journalists. Students in design fields compete for temporary employment in major metropolitan design centers, often willing to work for free in exchange for experience and impressive entries on their résumés. In 2013, a federal judge in New York charged that Fox Searchlight Pictures violated federal labor law and minimum wage laws by employing unpaid interns (Adams, 2013). A Supreme Court law from the 1940s describes a six-part test employers must meet to have unpaid workers. *Forbes* magazine cites the creative fields in particular as largely ignoring these laws, attracting more than a million students a year in unpaid labor seen to advance students' eventual search for full-time employment but also contributing to the billable hours of employers (Adams, 2013). In some cases, design employers have advertised these positions specifically as "apprenticeships," continuing low-wage or unpaid traditions of the field that preceded the availability of a college education in design.

A primary role of the guilds was to maintain high standards of craftsmanship at each threshold for advancement to master status. Across history, however, the very definition and status of "craft" have changed with the times. Art historian T. A. Heslop describes the emergence of a hierarchy between fine arts and craft in the twelfth century. The growth of consumer society and the apprenticeship system practiced by the guilds meant that craftsmen were no longer associated with major art patrons and resulting prestige (Heslop, 1997). Painters and sculptors rose in status as producing something only the wealthy or the church could afford, creating a distinction between fine and applied art that is reflected in today's art historical canon, separation of work in various types of museums (art versus craft, design, and historical institutions), and college curricula. This distinction between the creation of utilitarian, mass-produced objects and one-of-a-kind artistic expression is often the source of long-standing curricular disagreement among faculty, especially in colleges and universities where art and design reside in the same administrative unit and majors share first-year coursework.

The apprentice system also set the tone for the relationship between student and master that is reflected in some contemporary design classrooms. The task of the apprentice was to learn to produce work *in the style of the master.* High value was assigned to continuity among works produced by the same shop, regardless of individual makers. Today, it is possible to see this attitude reflected in "cult of personality" teaching, which produces visual similarity among student portfolios through faculty's art direction approach to instruction. The goal is less about developing independent styles and problem-solving than for students to walk in the shoes of the master.

THE ÉCOLE DES BEAUX-ARTS AND CLASSICAL EDUCATION IN ARCHITECTURE

An example of ongoing patronage for art and design can be found in the French royal academies. Louis XIV established academies in a variety of intellectual endeavors as a means of centralizing his power. Under the imprimatur of the Académie Royale d'Architecture, founded in 1671, prominent architects selected by the king met once a week to discuss ideas, address architectural problems, and advise the monarchy on royal buildings. As an extension of this work for royalty, members of the Academy lectured to the public and an elite group of students (called the éléve) twice a week on mathematics, geometry, and theories of architecture (Chafee, 1977). Unlike the medieval guilds, the Academy elevated the study of architecture from craft to philosophy and discourse, with a focus on beauty in the logic of classical buildings of ancient Rome and the Italian Renaissance (Chafee, 1977).

Decidedly aristocratic in membership and intent, the academies struggled under the French Revolution. In 1819, five years after the restoration of the monarchy, the individual academies devoted to painting, sculpture, and architecture were consolidated to form the École Royale des Beaux-Arts. However, architecture retained its own faculty and curriculum, and the École offered instruction in architecture continually until 1968, when student unrest at French universities resulted in protest for an "American-type" of architectural education (Davis, 2010).

The educational goal of the Academy throughout its history was to design in the tradition of great architects from the past and to appreciate the most perfect examples of architecture. Therefore, lectures and drawing exercises included detailed analyses of elements from exemplary buildings. The characteristics of the Beaux-Arts style of architecture included: symmetry; a single element as a defining gesture (such as a grand archway or colonnade); paired columns with entablatures (moldings and bands above the columns) that designated the location of columns; axial floor plans; and an articulated roofline that often included sculpture (Fricker & Fricker, 2010). In many Beaux-Arts buildings, long runs of steps led to the main entrance (Fricker & Fricker, 2010).

The course of study for mastering this style was a pyramid with four steps. At the base was preparation for admission, followed by second-class and first-class studies, and then competition for the Grand Prix de Rome at the peak (Chafee, 1977). Students progressed at their own rate, going as high in the curriculum as they could but with no guarantee of completion.

The student first found a master in an atelier, the independent workshop or studio of a professional architect. It was in the atelier that the applicant learned the practical work of architecture, which qualified him as an *aspirant à l'École des Beaux-Arts* through a letter of reference from the patron of the atelier. Under atelier patronage, aspirants typically spent two years preparing for the entrance exam, which included mathematics, geometry, history, drawings of architectural ornament, and architectural design (Chaffee, 1977). Aspirants had library and sketching privileges at the Academy and could sit for the exam, annually (later biannually) as many times as necessary, until they were thirty years old.

The second class consisted of lectures—also attended by aspirants—with no exams and no required attendance across the two to four years of study. Historically, students attended lectures on construction but ignored others (Chafee, 1977). The pedagogy for second-class study was the competition or *concours d'emulation* through which academy members judged student work (Salama, 1995). Most of these competitions evaluated architectural composition through timed sketches (one drawing after twelve hours of study) and rendered projects (three large drawings of a small building completed across two months) (Chafee, 1977). Four construction concours included work in stone, iron, wood, and an analysis of classical elements. Students could complete as many concours as they liked but were dropped if they completed none in any given year. Requirements changed over the years after study in architecture merged with the academies in painting and sculpture. There was increasing interest in figure drawing and ornament modeling, as well as concerns for mathematical and scientific proficiency (Chafee, 1977).

Advancement to the first class depended on receiving credit for all concours, as well as approval of two drawings based on an architectural program—one completed in twelve hours of isolation at the school and another refined in the atelier, then compared for the same idea to make sure they were done by the student and not the patron (Chafee, 1977). The first-class curriculum was similar to second-class study but emphasized six sketches and six rendered projects as part of the architecture concours.

The British envied the success of the French academies and established the Royal Academy in 1753. Like the French, the British saw drawing as a prerequisite to the development of design abilities across a range of industries (Puetz, 1999). British students learned through commercial drawing and model books. The former provided copying exercises, while the latter were collections of iconographic and formal elements from which students were expected to generate new compositions for various surfaces and materials (Puetz, 1999).

The École des Beaux-Arts established pedagogical practices we find in design education today, including the study of precedent and the use of important theoretical texts. François Blondell—the Academy's first professor and director—assembled the Academy's official syllabus from readings by selected authors. Blondell relied on Vitruvius, Palladio, Scamozzi, Vignola, Serlio, and Alberti (in that specific order), believing in the principles of antiquity rather than current practices in France. His public lectures focused on these readings and were published in three volumes: the first on the Five Orders of Architecture (Tuscan, Doric, Ionic, Corinthian, and Composite) and the second and third on a speculative rereading of ancient columns, pedestals, entablatures, architraves, and cornices (Gerbino, 2010).

This philosophical study of classical proportion and beauty was an attempt to define an ideal or "correct" architecture. Blondell's approach contrasted with that of the earlier craft-oriented guilds in which an understanding of built form developed through apprenticeships in local methods of construction and traditions of the regional culture (Gerbino, 2010). And while later academy directors countered that standards of beauty were changeable with the times, the curriculum remained focused on theories of architecture, traditional building materials, and studies of ancient precedents until modern construction in the first half of the twentieth century argued for a more technical education and presented practical competition from schools of engineering (Gerbino, 2010).

The Beaux-Arts interest in landmarks of antiquity influenced American architectural education, as well as the style of buildings at the end of the eighteenth and beginning of the nineteenth centuries. Thomas Jefferson, as minister to France, visited the Maison Carrée (ca. 20 BC), an example of Vitruvian architecture in Nimes, France. He commissioned a stucco model in the Beaux-Arts tradition of working from exemplars and used it as the basis for the design of the Virginia State Capitol Building (1785). Architecture was among the first academic disciplines at Jefferson's University of Virginia in 1819, elevating the field to the status of other kinds of intellectual inquiry. Jefferson's original campus design included ten pavilions—one for each academic college in ten different styles as an encyclopedia of architectural history—and a small version of the Roman Pantheon housing the library at the head of the axial layout. Jefferson said in a letter to James Madison, "How is public taste in this beautiful art to be cultivated in our countrymen unless we present to them, on every occasion when public buildings are to be erected, models for study and imitation" (Stapley quoting Jefferson, 1911).

If lectures were the place of Beaux-Arts discourse, the ateliers were the locus of practical study. Comprised of twenty to thirty students—usually in off-campus locations—ateliers were under the direction of professors or architects of distinction. The atelier was the precursor to the modern architectural studio in today's colleges and universities. Its practical content, pedagogy of active learning, and size were comparable to those of contemporary design classrooms. École students typically had the skills and knowledge to execute a variety of architecture styles, but the patron controlled the range of theories and form possible in student work. As with guild masters, the unstated intent in this instruction was to learn to design in the spirit of the patron's work. As mentioned earlier, this attitude still pervades much of contemporary design education, although many faculty are reluctant to admit it.

Atelier projects at the École des Beaux-Arts included school assignments and occasional commissions, but the dominant instructional format was competitions. The concours followed strict architectural programs and were juried by professionals, much as they are today. The highlight of École study was the Grand Prix de Rome, a nineteenth-century culmination of smaller competitions that populated the curriculum in the eighteenth century. It usually involved the design of a public building and secured four to five years of future study in Rome for the winner, as well as a contract for the building upon return to France. Many winners went on to become members of the Academy.

American universities began architectural education in earnest after the Civil War. American alumni of the École des Beaux-Arts established the

Society of Beaux-Arts Architects in 1894 to educate the nation's next generation of architects. Its professed values included re-creation of the French ateliers that supported the work of aspiring architects through study under accomplished professionals and juried competitions. The Society published and administered its own competitions through architectural schools, such as Columbia University and Massachusetts Institute of Technology. Most American schools adopted the École des Beaux-Arts curricular content and practices, including the Paris Prize as a corollary to the Prix de Rome.

This legacy of juried competitions as curricular content is still apparent in architectural education. Unlike other design disciplines, in which competitions are often poorly organized and utilize a client strategy to circumvent professional fees for design services, architectural competitions often produce strong work and publish outcomes that inform the field. The Beaux-Arts jury system is also still used in end-of-semester reviews, although the psychological stress of this system is the subject of recent criticism in studies such as Kathryn Anthony's *Design Juries on Trial* (see chapter 5).

INDUSTRY AND INDEPENDENT SCHOOLS
OF DESIGN IN THE UNITED STATES

The Industrial Revolution (1760–1840) provided a new impetus for design education. In 1837, the British House of Commons established a committee to "inquire into the best means of extending a knowledge of the Arts and the Principles of Design among the people (especially the manufacturing population) of the country" (Cole, 1853). The result was the development of Government Schools of Design, beginning in London at Somerset House and duplicated in twenty-one other locations in Great Britain. In his opening address in Westminster, Sir Henry Cole described the purpose of the institution:

> . . . to provide for the architect, the upholsterer, the weaver, the printer, the potter, and all manufacturers, artizans better educated to originate and execute their respective wares, and to invest them with greater symmetry of form, with increased harmony of colour, and with greater fitness of decoration; to render manufacturers not less useful by ornamenting them, but more beautiful, and therefore more useful (Cole, 1853).

The design school movement also flourished in the United States, although under the auspices of industry itself rather than government. In the second half of the nineteenth century, the expense of importing decorative products from Europe—china, wallpaper, textiles, and furniture—pushed American industry to find homegrown solutions for satisfying the public appetite for well-designed products of the Industrial Age. Only the wealthy could afford British and French designs. American manufacturers bought European patterns for duplication in an attempt to lower costs, but the long-term response to growing middle-class markets appeared to lie in cultivating design talent at home (De Angeli Walls, 2001). Governing boards of these new college-level design schools saw the work of their graduates as enlightening the populace in standards of "good taste" through an education that encouraged European approaches to form (De Angeli Walls, 2001). Philanthropists and manufacturers determined appropriate curricular content, and their interests reflected growing separation between fine arts and design.

American interest in design education also coincided with increasing concern for the issues of class presented by immigration in the late 1800s. Twelve million immigrants entered the United States between 1870 and 1900, with 70 percent coming through New York and competing for survival through lower-class employment as servants and factory workers (Library of Congress, 2016). Society presented limited employment opportunities for middle-class women needing to support themselves through labor matched to their higher social status. Design offered a viable alternative.

This confluence of forces resulted in a collection of schools in the United States created by businessmen, in part to educate women in design and as art teachers for public schools that would guarantee continuing skills for expanding industry.

Philadelphia School of Design

Of the original efforts to develop design education opportunities for women, only the 1853 Philadelphia School of Design—now Moore College of Art—remains devoted exclusively to women's education. Early criteria for the admission of women signaled the bias of their benefactors—native birth, some previous education, churchgoing Protestant faith, and no male breadwinner in the family—and the institution enforced a strong code of conduct for admitted students (De Angeli Walls, 2001). Under a post–Civil War agreement with the State of Pennsylvania in exchange for public funds, the Philadelphia School of Design also established the Pittsburgh School of Design, which merged in 1902 with Carnegie Institute of Technology—now Carnegie Mellon University.

The New England School of Design

At the urging of the Massachusetts state legislature, the New England School of Design opened in 1851 as one of three schools, including the Massachusetts Institute of Technology. Lacking sufficient funding from an industrial sponsor, the school closed during tough economic times but reopened in 1873 as the Massachusetts Normal Art School, a coeducational institution under support from textile mill owners and railroad families. Its purpose was to train drawing teachers for the public schools, as well as architects and designers. Now called the Massachusetts College of Art and Design, the school is the only publicly funded, freestanding college of art and design in the United States.

Cooper Union

Cooper Union began as the New York School of Design for Women in 1852, offering tuition-free classes in "drawing for mechanical purposes and in designing for paper, cotton, and woolen manufacturers" (De Angeli Walls, 2001, p. 6). In 1859, industrialist Peter Cooper funded the institution as a center for the study of architecture, art, and engineering. The school served as an expression of Cooper's progressive social views, accepting students of color and housing a public reading room for the children of New York.

Maryland Institute College of Art

Maryland Institute College of Art started as the Maryland Institute for the Promotion of Mechanical Arts. Its charter described a mission to:

> encourage and promote the Manufactures and the Mechanic and useful Arts, by the establishment of popular lectures . . . a library and cabinets of models and minerals; by offering premiums for excellence in those branches of National Industry deemed worthy of

encouragement; by examining new inventions . . . and by such other means as experience may suggest (Maryland Institute College of Art, 2016)

The institute operated a night school in 1849 to supply the printing industry and growing industrial design market with skilled artisans. The women's Day School for Design at Maryland Institute followed in 1854 and included teacher-training programs and study in applied arts. Publishers and wallpaper and textile manufacturers purchased student designs, a common practice in early design schools that helped women to fund their education.

Rhode Island School of Design

It took Rhode Island School of Design two decades from planning to offering its first classes to men and women in 1878. The Women's Pavilion at the 1876 Centennial Exposition in Philadelphia asserted women's rights to self-sufficiency and highlighted the work and patents of women in American design schools. The ladies of the Rhode Island Centennial Committee had $1,675 left over following the exposition and chose a board of trustees to found a design school (Barrett & Martinez, 2008). The Rhode Island General Assembly incorporated the institution under a purpose described first as instruction of "artisans in drawing, painting, modeling, and designing, that they may successfully apply the principles of Art to the requirements of trade and manufacture" (Barrett & Martinez, 2008, p. 31). They also charged the school with the general advancement of public art education and the practice of art.

Later than the northeastern schools, other independent art schools also opened under funding from philanthropists interested in design.

Cranbrook Academy of Art

Cranbrook Academy of Art was established by publishers George Gough and Ellen Scripps Booth, who hired Finnish architect Eliel Saarinen to design the academy as one of several institutions on a 319-acre educational campus north of Detroit. Receiving approval to offer college degrees in 1932, the Booths chose Eliel Saarinen's son, Eero, as the academy's first president and charged him with the mission to influence the quality of American products and architecture "in the Arts and Crafts tradition." Faculty and alumni included Charles and Ray Eames, Florence Knoll, and Harry Bertoia, who contributed to the growth of the modern furniture industry in Michigan.

California College of the Arts

Frederick Meyer—a cabinetmaker from Germany also involved in the Arts and Crafts movement—founded the California College of the Arts. Meyer set up shop in the Bay Area in 1902. When an earthquake destroyed his business, he started the California Guild of Arts and Crafts with $45, forty-three students, and three teachers (California College of the Arts, 2016). Across time, he added courses in wood design, glass, and interior architecture.

Art Center College of Design

Art Center College of Design owes its beginnings to Edward A. "Tink" Adams, an advertising man whose goal was to prepare designers for leadership roles in advertising, publishing, and industrial design (Art Center, 2016). Adams served as the first director and committed to staffing the school through a faculty of working design professionals, a tradition that remains characteristic of the institution today.

Direct connections within industry and a curricular focus on design subjects, therefore, established leadership roles for these colleges in the preparation of professional designers in the United States. For many decades it was difficult for university programs in graphic, industrial, and interior design to compete with the professional approach to design study offered by these institutions. Locations in major metropolitan design centers, frequent student commissions under professional sponsors, and academic schedules that encouraged apprenticeships while in school ensured an easy transition from school to practice for art and design school graduates. Today, independent art and design schools still identify themselves as members of a distinct educational group. The Association of Independent Colleges of Art and Design (AICAD) includes forty-three schools in the United States and Canada, forty-one of which are single-discipline institutions.

New industrial production methods at the turn of the century also redefined the notion of craft in design. The assembly line reconfigured traditional handicraft processes as a series of simplified steps, creating a new mission and teaching opportunities for industrial arts in public schools (De Angeli Walls, 2001). Under these conditions, students who struggled with drawing as fine artists could still learn to draft in ways acceptable to industry. The early decades of the twentieth century marked the emergence of specialized training for art teachers, and there is a strong history of art requirements in the public-school curricula of states where these art and design colleges are located.

The development of drawing schools in the nineteenth century also served the need for preparation in architectural drawing. The Franklin Institute of the State of Pennsylvania enrolled young men "to promote useful arts by diffusing a knowledge of mechanical science" and sought "to improve the conditions and elevate the character of the operative class of society, by affording them the only effectual means for this purpose, education" (Cohen, 1994, p. 142). Drawing schools offered courses throughout the 1800s; however, the turn of the century saw growth in university offerings in architecture, and drawing school education became preliminary study for later college education or vocational training for drafting positions. Consistent with a growing sense of the modern age, society sought broader educational approaches that met ambitions for the emerging professions of the twentieth century.

THE MODERNIST AGENDA OF THE BAUHAUS

Although the Bauhaus is probably the best-known twentieth-century approach to design education, its origins were a response to the nineteenth-century effects of the Industrial Revolution and emerging conditions of the modern world. The Arts and Crafts movement in Great Britain (1880–1910) was a backlash to the poor quality and faux materials of machine-manufactured products at the turn of the century, but its return to handcrafted objects was an economic and social failure. Its artisan guilds and hand processes were too labor intensive to meet the growing demands of everyday citizens for household goods.

In 1896, the German government sent architect Hermann Muthesius to study British residential architecture and design. Admiring the understated functionality and honesty to materials in Arts and Crafts housing and products, Muthesius recommended in his three-volume report on *Das Englische Haus* (*The English House*, 1904–1905) installing art-oriented workshops in his country's handicraft schools (Droste, 2006). However, unlike the British Arts and Crafts movement's rejection of commercial manufacturing, the Germans embraced machine production and new styles that would reflect their industrial prowess.

The Deutscher Werkbund (German Association of Craftsmen) was founded in 1907 in Munich with the aim of cooperation among "art, industry, and crafts in the enablement of commercial activity by means of education, propaganda, and a united stand on pertinent questions" (Droste, 2006, p. 12, quoting from Heinrich Waentig, 1907). Commercial companies participated in the Werkbund and employed its designers, including architects Peter Behrens (the Werkbund's first president) and Walter Gropius. The Werkbund organized exhibitions, published professional work, and influenced curriculum in German art schools.

The Weimar Bauhaus (1919–1925)

By 1917, Walter Gropius had become disenchanted with the Werkbund's rigid interpretation of design for industry and turned his attention to opening a new school that advocated for artistic expression in design (Aynsley, 2009). Following failed proposals to establish a postsecondary institution that provided artistic advice to industry, he was eventually hired by the government in 1919 to head two struggling schools—the Weimar School of Arts and Crafts and the Weimar Academy of Fine Arts—under a single title, Staatliches Bauhaus (State School of Building). This consolidation allowed Gropius to restructure education around modern ideas of art school reform—which called for handicraft as the foundation of art education and governance by a council of masters—without undermining existing institutions by establishing an entirely new school (Droste, 2006).

Gropius's curricular plan reconciled previously separate arts disciplines and leveled class differences, assigning the craftsman and the artist equal status in instruction. He wrote, ". . . we must all return to the crafts! . . . The artist is an exalted craftsman . . . a foundation in handcraft is essential for every artist" (Wingler, 1969, p. 31). In the guild tradition, entering students were called *apprentices* and advanced to *journeyman* status as they progressed through the curriculum. In the first class of 150 students, nearly half were women, but by 1920, Gropius suggested a more rigorous review of female applicants. He eventually sent women straight to the weaving workshop to avoid what he dismissed as overly feminine work in the other workshops (Droste, 2006;

Aynsley, 2009). The school employed the most notable artists of the time as masters of form—including Lyonel Feininger, Johannes Itten, Wassily Kandinsky, Paul Klee, and Oskar Schlemmer—but Gropius admitted having difficulty in finding artisans who could teach as masters of craft (Droste, 2006).

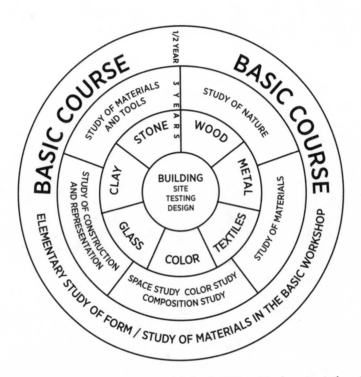

FIGURE 1.1 *Walter Gropius's 1922 plan for the Weimer Bauhaus curriculum (translated from the original German version in the Bauhaus statutes). It is easy to see in the plan the emphasis on elements and principles of design and mastery of materials that many college-level foundation programs and secondary art education curricula replicated for much of the twentieth century. Absent is the study of theory and history that both preceded the Bauhaus approach to education and followed in the curriculum at the Ulm School of Design.*

The Weimar Bauhaus curriculum included a preliminary course (Vorkurs) taken by all students and workshops focused on particular media or project types (Figure 1.1). The Vorkurs under Johannes Itten was the mainstay of the Weimar curriculum. Studies were divided into three areas: natural objects and materials; analysis of the Old Masters; and life drawing (Droste, 2006). The study of nature and materials was to illustrate the "essential and contradictory" qualities of each (Wingler, 1969, p. 280) (Figure 1.2). Theories of form assigned a particular character to each elementary geometric shape, with contrast in color, rhythm, and shape as recurring themes of investigation. Unlike the copying exercises of the École des Beaux-Arts, Bauhaus analyses of Old Masters explored essential concepts (line, movement, contrast, etc.), which students were asked to discover through analytical drawings. Life drawing from models focused on rhythm in the human form. Itten also emphasized development of the inner being, starting his classes with breathing exercises as a way of discovering internal rhythm and subjective experience (Droste, 2006).

FIGURE 1.2 *Edna Lawrence Nature Lab at Rhode Island School of Design, photography by Jo Sittenfeld. Opened in 1937 as an essential part of the early RISD foundation curriculum, the lab continues to serve as inspiration for students across art and design disciplines in the college.*

Gropius and the Council of Masters monitored the six-hour workshop experiences with the goal of integrating theory and practice, imagination and technical skills, although later critiques of the approach cite a lack of substantive theoretical discussion and reading as a limitation of the Bauhaus curriculum. Each workshop had a master of form and a master of craft. The curriculum included workshops in joinery, pottery, mural painting, textiles, metals, furniture, bookbinding, and graphic printing. Gropius hoped to establish an architecture department in Weimar but met resistance from the government (Droste, 2006). He arranged for students to spend some time at a civil engineering school in the area, and there was a brief period of study under his architecture partner Adolf Meyer in 1920, but there was never a curricular emphasis on the subject in the early Bauhaus years.

Gropius and Itten disagreed on the practice of engaging students in commissions, one of many internal conflicts in Bauhaus history. Itten believed the purpose of a Bauhaus education was to develop harmony between the individual personality and his or her surroundings, while Gropius saw interaction with the commercial world of industry as a fundamental purpose of the curriculum. The disagreement reached a climax when Gropius asked students in the joinery workshop to design seating for a theater, renovated under Gropius's architectural practice with Adolf Meyer (Droste, 2006). Itten resigned in protest, arguably removing a curricular obstacle to the creation of products that suited industrial production. Although Itten's successors retained the core principles of the original Vorkurs, they dropped his emphasis on spiritual and personality development, which proved increasingly difficult to justify to government sources of the school's funding (Aynsley, 2009).

Gropius's interest in commissions was not only philosophical. The Bauhaus relationship with state government was tenuous at best. Paid commissions lessened the institution's dependency on public subsidies. A government loan required the school to show its accomplishments in a 1923 exhibition, presenting an opportunity to publicize Bauhaus ideas for new products with a wider audience. The exhibition included some of the first standardized housing designs and an example of a fully furnished residence that used new building materials and techniques. Gropius explored the potential of establishing a company to market Bauhaus products but failed to implement the strategy in Weimar (Droste, 2006). However, he did manage to hire new faculty—such as Laszlo Moholy-Nagy—who showed interest in the relationships among design, technology, and the new materials of commercial production.

Commercial projects in the workshops shifted the Bauhaus curriculum toward designing for industrial manufacturing and away from its origins in handcrafted form and drawing. Josef Albers was hired to teach the Vorkurs with Moholy-Nagy in 1923 and later in Dessau. He extended the preliminary course to six months and included student visits to factories as part of the curriculum. Albers systematized the study of commercial materials, asking students to progress through glass, paper, and metal in a deliberate order and to produce no waste. He would leave students in the workshop, each with a single sheet of paper and no tools, only to return hours later expecting new forms that optimized the inherent properties of the medium. Gerhard Marck's pottery workshop used cast forms suitable for mass production, rather than hand-built methods that resulted in one-of-a-kind products. The textile workshop collaborated with the furniture workshop and sold reproduction rights to students' fabric and carpet designs. Under Gropius as the master of form, Bauhaus furniture had to address the practical criteria favored by consumers: no heavy dust-collecting cushions, an angled position for the upper half of the body, and the application of color to emphasize methods of construction (Droste, 2006). After 1921, the graphic printing workshop became a production shop devoted almost entirely to commissions, including a portfolio of new European prints that was issued regularly until 1924.

Despite efforts to be self-sustaining and to stay out of politics, the Weimar Bauhaus finally succumbed to the opposition of right-wing conservatives in government, who accused the school of Communist tendencies and argued for its closing in 1924. Gropius was terminated, and the masters declared their contracts dissolved in a January 1925 protest letter, with no long-range plan for reestablishing the school (Wingler, 1969). Although the school had strong industrial endorsement, external resources were insufficient to maintain operation without government support.

The Dessau Bauhaus (1925–1932)

After the school's closing in Weimar, the city of Dessau—an urban center for engineering—expressed interest in the Bauhaus. Following successful negotiations to join the Bauhaus with existing craft and trade schools under Gropius's direction, the former state-supported institution was reestablished under municipal support. Initially located in an old department store, the Dessau Bauhaus opened a new complex in 1926. The workshops designed all the furnishings for new faculty housing, and Gropius finally established his long-planned limited company with a catalog of Bauhaus products.

Between 1925 and 1927, Gropius focused on a new curriculum. He raised the status of the institution to a Hochschule für Gestaltung (Institute of Design)—authorizing it to award diplomas—and dropped the designation of *apprentices, journeymen,* and *masters* in favor of *students* and *professors.* He reduced the number of workshops and organized them under departments. The architecture department was the last to be established but soon formed the hub around which other workshops operated. Under the direction of Swiss architect Hannes Meyer, the architecture curriculum included two tracks: building *(bau)* and interior decoration *(inneneinrichtung).* Study was supported by workshops in metals, textiles, joinery, and mural painting. Advertising was the second department in the school's hierarchy—a reconfiguration of the old printing workshop—and now included sculpture and photography workshops in addition to work in book design.

Albers, Moholy-Nagy, Klee, and Kandinsky taught the Vorkurs. Albers continued his systematic exploration of materials, while Moholy-Nagy concentrated on spatial organization in three dimensions with an emphasis on achieving more with less (Wingler, 1969). Klee directed the second semester with focus on a theory of pictorial form and color, starting with a systematic exploration of black-and-white scales that can still be found in today's foundation coursework. Kandinsky also taught color and analytical drawing, favoring subjects that could be simplified as geometric forms in minimalist compositions (Wingler, 1969).

The advertising program saw the greatest transformation under Bauhaus alumnus Herbert Bayer. Previously a production center, emphasis in the workshop shifted to creative work as a precursor to the modern practice of graphic design. The workshop designed all of the Bauhaus publications under Bayer's art direction. Bayer and Moholy-Nagy introduced new sans-serif typography and the use of photography, while at the same time emphasizing respect for the author's content (Wingler, 1969). Students also studied theories of advertising and its effects on audiences.

Gunta Stölzl directed the textile workshop, where work moved toward commercial production techniques. The weaving workshop went from producing artistic carpets to utilitarian floor coverings (Droste, 2006). Production processes were systematized, and students undertook the full range of commercial activities necessary to bring textiles to market. They studied color and patterning under Klee.

The joinery workshop was under the direction of Marcel Breuer, who pioneered the use of tubular steel in furniture but retained licensing of his own designs. There was an emphasis on function, economy, and how furniture fit with home interiors. New equipment allowed students to explore industrial manufacturing processes and materials not previously used in furniture.

Although the curricular link to commerce seemed better resolved than in Weimar, the Dessau Bauhaus under Gropius was not without conflict. Younger and older faculty argued over pay equity (Droste, 2006). Professors disagreed about the direction of workshops, the role of art in the curriculum, and whether the design process should begin with elementary forms and primary colors, the industrial machine, or social and scientific concerns (Droste, 2006). Although the city of Dessau provided modest financial support, its conservative leaders refused to increase funding to the school, and other revenues from commercial production failed to fill the gap. Bauhaus work was seen as too modern for consumers' taste and too unresolved for mass production (Droste, 2006). Gropius had enough of the constant turmoil and resigned in 1928 to return to full-time architectural practice. Bayer, Breuer, and Moholy-Nagy left the school with Gropius, creating another opening for curriculum revision by those who followed.

Hannes Meyer replaced Gropius as director and served until 1930, reorganizing the Bauhaus curriculum under ongoing pressure for austerity. Meyer differed philosophically with Gropius. His priority in design was meeting everyday human needs and serving the social good, not universal form or the study of nature as espoused by Gropius. He extended the length of the preliminary course under Albers, Klee, and Kandinsky. Scientific and social criteria received equal curricular attention with other aspects of the design process, much to the disappointment of Albers and Kandinsky, whose philosophical positions were supported by vocal student advocates.

Meyer consolidated workshops and published a set of principles for their operation, promoting cost efficiency, self-administration, and production-oriented teaching (Droste, 2006). Each workshop had a head, master craftsman, and paid student assistant. Meyer also established the dominant role of architecture in the school. Architectural theory was taught over four semesters and addressed the design of environmental systems and technical drawing, often taught by engineers. Architecture, according to Meyer, was the obvious result of careful analysis and scientific study. Student work included charts and graphs, reflecting a departure from Gropius's primary interest in form. "Vertical work gangs" grouped students at different levels for commissioned work (Droste, 2006). The development of the individual architect was far less important than a collective effort to meet social needs.

Meyer also made changes in the financial operations of the institution. Believing in the integration of the school with society, he opened admission to nonvisual students, increasing enrollment from 150 to 200 students and raising student revenues. He successfully negotiated contracts with industry for lamps, wallpaper, advertising, and exhibition design, although the income from these activities was not enough to make the school self-sustaining.

By 1930, Meyer had completely transformed the curriculum to one producing design that was "... practical, purely rational ..." (Wingler, 1969, p. 527). His efforts to establish new principles and growing political dissent, however, polarized the student body. By 1930, a Communist cell of students had attracted the attention of the right-wing press in Dessau, and the mayor called for Meyer's dismissal. Albers and Kandinsky fueled the controversy, worried over Meyer's diminishing interest in the artistic part of the Vorkurs (Wingler, 1969).

At the suggestion of Gropius, the government opened discussions with architect Ludwig Mies van der Rohe, who eventually took over as director amidst student protest of Meyer's dismissal and an investigation by the Council of Masters to name the Communist sympathizers. In 1930, with the consent of the mayor, the Council of Masters called for closure of the school, "readmission" of former students, and expulsion of Meyer's defenders. Students were removed from any role in the institution's governance and had to sign a constitution that prohibited them from engaging in any political activity (Droste, 2006). By 1931, however, the National Socialist German Workers' Party—commonly referred to as the "Nazi Party"—gained control of the city council and moved to close the school permanently.

The Berlin Bauhaus (1932–1933)

Mies rented an old factory in Berlin, enlisted students to renovate its interior, and launched a new curriculum in 1932. He reduced studies to six semesters and reinvented the institution as a school of architecture surrounded by a constellation of smaller workshops in other areas. He required the Vorkurs only for students who lacked sufficient training from previous studies or work (Droste, 2006). Under Mies's administration, the Bauhaus behaved like a school with an emphasis on teaching. "Practical experience (working on actual construction)" was done during holidays and on students' own time (Wingler, 1969, p. 183). Although the workshops produced prototypes for industry, production was no longer part of the curriculum.

Mies's architecture curriculum was divided into three stages. In the first stage, students learned technical fundamentals, as well as building law, statistics, mathematics, and physics (Droste, 2006). This instruction was compulsory and often taught by engineers. The second stage addressed apartment and town planning, envisioning a "new city" for German society. Mies taught the third stage in which drawing was essential to the intellectual and artistic pursuit of architecture. Architecture was "confrontation with space, proportion, and material," not the social and practical discipline promoted by Meyer (Droste, 2006, p. 213).

Mies's shift to a predominantly academic model for curriculum meant that students had fewer means for earning money. At the same time, dramatic reduction in public funding—owing largely to political opposition from the National Socialists—resulted in the Bauhaus purchasing student designs for later commercialization. Students who objected to this practice were expelled.

The Gestapo closed the school in 1933, acting on Nazi opinion that the school was "unGerman," too modern in its philosophy, and a front for Communists and foreign radicals (Droste, 2006). Hitler's preference for Neo-classical architecture of monumental proportions ran counter to Bauhaus principles. Mies protested and the school reopened again, but the faculty and Mies eventually voted to close less than a year after moving to Berlin from Dessau.

The Bauhaus in America

World War II facilitated the spread of Bauhaus influence in the United States. As the climate for modern design grew more hostile in Europe, a number of Bauhaus masters left Germany for America. In 1933, architect and Museum of Modern Art curator Philip Johnson encouraged Josef Albers to head a new college at Black Mountain, North Carolina. Albers remained there as head of the painting program until 1949 when he moved to Yale. The school adopted the progressive educational philosophy of pragmatist John Dewey in which art and design were central to study in the liberal arts. American graphic designer Alvin Lustig and architect Buckminster Fuller were included in an impressive roster of artists and designers who delivered an interdisciplinary course of study at the rural North Carolina college. Although the school closed in 1957, many important artists and designers passed through the institution in its twenty-four-year history, and its experimental liberal arts approach to curriculum continues to be a source of study for scholars today.

Ludwig Mies van der Rohe immigrated to Chicago, where he became the director of the School of Architecture at Armour Institute, now called Illinois Institute of Technology. In 1937, at the invitation of Walter Paepcke, chairman of the Container Corporation of America, Laszlo Moholy-Nagy also moved to Chicago and was appointed director of the New Bauhaus. The Institute of Design merged with Illinois Institute of Technology in 1949. Like the German model, the first year of study included a preliminary course based in drawing and disciplined explorations in materials and techniques. Students specialized in the second year, with the photography program under Hungarian György Kepes—who immigrated to the United States in 1937 after work with Moholy-Nagy in Berlin and London—being the most notable in the early years of the institution.

Walter Gropius and Marcel Breuer went to teach at the Harvard Graduate School of Design (GSD), where Gropius chaired the Architecture Department from 1937 to 1952. They instituted a Bauhaus pedagogy—shifting Harvard's study of architecture from one based on classical form and the Beaux-Arts style to one based on modernism—but they were unable to establish the workshops from the German curriculum. Gropius had a falling out with Joseph Hudnut, the GSD dean, over the International Style. Hudnut felt the rigid modernist agenda "was draining the life from cities" (Loeffler, 2002). He also believed in a strong liberal education, including history, which Gropius thought could suffocate individual creativity (Loeffler, 2002). The tension between the two grew, and Gropius resigned in 1952. Architectural historian Anthony Alofsin describes the dispute as "a fault line at the center of modernism that critically impeded America's wholesale adoption of European avant-garde ideas" (Read, 2005, p. 117).

Yale University established the first graphic design degree program with formation of a Department of Design in 1950 under the chairmanship of Josef Albers, who was given complete freedom to hire faculty without the approval of tenured professors (Kelly, 2001). The stated purpose by Dean Charles Sawyer was to disassociate the program from fine arts and form a closer identity with architecture (Kelly, 2001). Although the program began as a four-year undergraduate degree, Yale soon converted the curricular offering to a master of fine arts. Alvin Eisenman led the graphic design program for forty years (1950–1990), attracting teachers from Europe and establishing a faculty exchange with the Royal College of Art in London. Herbert Matter, Armin Hofmann, Wolfgang Weingart, and Alexey Brodovitch, as well as noted

American designers Paul Rand and Lester Beall, played important roles in defining American modernism through graduates of the school as well as their own professional work.

The influx of designers and teachers from Europe ensured the modernist influence of the Bauhaus on design education in the United States. Dietmar Winkler, a design professor born and educated in Germany, described the Bauhaus as providing educators with a rational language of form and tools well matched to arguments for the effectiveness of visual concepts with clients and critics (Winkler, 1997). The Vorkurs was—and still is in many colleges and universities—the model for the foundation year of art and design study. So strong is the Bauhaus impact on first-year curricula that many schools still resist any challenge by alternative approaches arguably better suited to contemporary times. Under this application of Bauhaus projects, there is an assumption that design study begins with abstraction and that any design problem can be resolved through form alone. Regrettably, bits and pieces of Itten's and Albers's preliminary course exercises are often disconnected from critical examination of their origins in modernist philosophy or the carefully scaffolded coursework that surrounded original assignments.

Winkler articulated the dilemma of the narrow limits of Bauhaus investigations when considering the processes of communication. He described contemporary design problems as requiring "awareness not just of visual perception and visual discrimination but also of the total ecology of valuation, value discrimination, identity, territoriality, status, and anything that influences and alters humans' social and personal behaviour" (Winkler, 1997, p. 129). He challenged the status of the German school in design history, categorizing it as a trade or craft school and its faculty as restricted by their own ideology and undiluted purpose in influencing industry: "The students' education was seriously lacking in intellectual stimuli; no theory was taught, no economic or political history, no natural or social sciences, no music, no formal art history, and no literature" (Winkler, 1997, pp. 130–131).

Winkler attributes the vocational orientation of many master's design programs in the United States to the prewar integration of Bauhaus curriculum with the liberal arts culture of Ivy League schools, intended to support the Allied demand for applied research (Winkler, 1997). Not long after, many state universities developed design programs and copied the Ivy League model. As a result, most design master's programs in the United States are places to refine professional skills learned in undergraduate education, not to learn new skills in research or to engage in intellectual discourse about the social consequences of design action.

The preliminary course at the Bauhaus also influenced the content of art education in K–12 schools. Art education professor Arthur Efland describes the adoption of Bauhaus pedagogy by art teachers as predicated on a "general conviction that the elements of design were the underlying basis for all of the arts" and that they were "discoveries one made through the investigation of materials" (Efland, 1990, p. 218). This approach was consistent with modern philosophy to reject all previous styles under a seemingly neutral exploration of form and to standardize the approach to solving problems, regardless of their content and context. In this way, the curriculum of the Vorkurs offered a system for teaching basics that could be encouraged through the preservice education of art teachers and duplicated in schools around the country. Although some K–12 art teachers today purport to teach design as part of the visual arts curriculum, many focus on the arrangement of form in objects that secondarily have utilitarian purposes. It is difficult, for example, to find discussions of users or context in these investigations. In a study by the National Endowment for the Arts of how teachers integrate design in K–12 classrooms, art teachers were the most confused among teachers of all subjects regarding the potential of design to connect learning to the world outside of school (Davis et al., 1997). Science and social studies teachers had more robust definitions of design that placed form and process in service to other concepts.

The location of many graphic, industrial, and interior design programs in departments or schools of art (rather than engineering, architecture, or a free-standing college of design) is the reflection of a Bauhaus philosophy that unified the arts under a single program of study. As discussed in later chapters of this book, this arts-based location of design programs often presents challenges for curricula under more recent priorities for the study of design. And although the engagement of students in sponsored commissions predates the Bauhaus, the practice of long-term affiliation of design programs with commercial companies can be attributed to early practices by the German school.

THE ULM SCHOOL OF DESIGN AND A CURRICULUM OF SOCIAL RESPONSIBILITY

After the chaos of World War II, a small group of designers in Germany longed for an education that addressed the contribution of design to rebuilding a productive and socially responsible nation. Otl Aicher, Inge Scholl, and Max Bill confronted not only the physical ruins of European industry but also clear evidence that previous intellectual traditions and pride in culture had prevented everyday Germans from resisting the Nazis (Müller & Spitz, 2014). They founded the Ulm School of Design with the express intent of designing products and information that were practical, affordable, and honest in their appearance as essential to rebuilding postwar society, both economically and socially.

The Nazis had murdered nonviolent resisters Hans and Sophie Scholl, siblings of Inge Scholl and friends of her husband Otl Aicher, making the designers suspicious of government. The school began as a private institution with the intent of not accepting municipal or state support. Financial backing came through a matching one-million-mark grant from two Americans: US High Commissioner for Occupied Germany John McCloy and journalist Shepard Stone, who went on to direct the Aspen Institute of Humanistic Studies in Berlin. However, to achieve the match, Scholl's foundation eventually accepted city and government support (Lindinger, 1991).

After offering adult education lectures by philosophers and theologians in the late 1940s, the school opened in 1953 with four-year diploma study as a center for teaching and research in the design of products (for domestic, industrial, and scientific use) and information for mass media (Lindinger, 1991). The program of study included four departments: Product Design, Visual Communication, Building, and Information. Roughly half of the students were international, and the faculty included scientists and designers, including former Bauhaus instructors. Max Bill—a Swiss architect, industrial designer, and graphic designer with Bauhaus roots—became the first rector of a campus built purposefully for the school's curriculum.

The Ulm Hochschule für Gestaltung offered a curriculum focused on the designer's social responsibility and a rational design process. The curriculum challenged modernist beliefs that every design problem could be solved through the examination and simplification of properties inherent in the object, its obvious function, and its production. Aicher felt that culture included all mechanically produced objects and everyday actions (Müller & Spitz, 2014). Therefore, design demanded careful consideration of context and methods that reflected an objective, multidisciplinary perspective. Design was to embrace a systems approach—not one-of-a-kind objects with an Arts and Crafts bias—and form was to be timeless, not driven by consumer taste or style. A 1956 prospectus described design as having "nothing to do with vagaries of fashion or the unrelenting search for new effect . . . The development of an object requires intensive research and methodological work" (Wingler, 1969, p. 575).

Although Ulm faculty rejected Walter Gropius's suggestion that the school be named "Ulm Bauhaus," Max Bill's Bauhaus education from 1927 to 1929 formed a link between the Basic Course at Ulm and the Vorkurs at the Bauhaus. In the early years of the school, a concern for mathematics and geometry in the Basic Course was reminiscent of the Bauhaus curriculum. For Aicher and his colleagues, however, the Bauhaus had negative connotations in its lack of interest in the role of culture as everyday experience. In developing the Ulm curriculum, faculty rejected the study of painting, sculpture, and aesthetics as an end in itself. Aicher said, "He who has nothing to say looks for style, he who lives by materialism worships the mind, he who does business patronizes culture" (Lindinger, 1991, p. 125). In other words, the Ulm faculty saw design as "counter-art, a work of civilization, a civilizing culture" in postwar Europe (Lindinger, 1991, p. 125). Aicher found the criteria for design in the specific tasks it had to perform in a concrete world, not in universal and purely abstract form.

Aicher and theorist Tomas Maldonado consistently advocated for departing from the craft-based curriculum of the Bauhaus in favor of science and analytical studies (Lindinger, 1991). This rejection of Bill's art-oriented philosophy resulted in his resignation in 1956. Maldonado replaced Bill and transformed the curriculum under his preference for theory over practice. The curriculum of the next two years strengthened the connections between design, science, and technology. It was during this time that "The Ulm Model" emerged as a multidisciplinary approach—including scientists, researchers, technicians, and salespeople—with an emphasis on social responsibility (Lindinger, 1991). Design was based on a rational methodology, "an unprejudiced and thorough examination of the context of a problem, objective evaluation, and weighing of the analysis results" (Müller & Spitz, 2014, p. 32).

Maldonado reoriented the Basic Course, adding studies in perceptual science and semiotics. Annenberg School of Communication professor Klaus Krippendorf cites Ulm as the first design school to recognize the science of signs as an area of study (Krippendorf, 2006). Maldonado subscribed to the theories of Charles Morris, who described symbols as having three types of relationships: semantic, syntactic, and pragmatic. Krippendorff criticizes this taxonomical approach to science as resisting validation. "Vocabularies took the place of unchallengeable truths" (Krippendorff, 2006, p. 306). Although many of today's communication design programs teach aspects of semiotics—often favoring the work of Morris and American philosopher Charles Sanders Peirce—it is not clear how many of these programs use semiotic concepts beyond discussions of historical theory.

Between 1958 and 1962, Maldonado's emphasis on theory and the social sciences, research, planning, and technology grew. The Basic Course still involved the study of form and work with different materials, but investigations expanded to include the social and political issues of the times, criticism, and deeper understanding of the role of science and technology. Scientists soon outnumbered designers on the faculty, including mathematician and planning theorist Horst Rittel, known for coining the term *wicked problems*—ill-resolved social challenges in which knowledge alone is insufficient to the task, a plurality of objectives resists a singular solution, and every problem is a symptom of another problem (Rittel and Webber, 1973). Rittel is credited with framing a science of design and the development of operational research methods at Ulm and later at the University of California, Berkeley. He described design as argument among experts in different fields, rather than a linear process directed at simple problems and solutions. For Rittel, design was political, deliberative, and concerned with instrumental knowledge; "how what-is relates to what-ought-to-be" (Dubberly & Rith, 2007, p. 73).

The growth in scientific positivism resulted in tension among the designers and scientists. For some students and faculty, the study of planning methods overtook concerns for innovation. Notions of a value-free, objective form of design raised "questions of morality, aesthetics, and normative values" among the designers and even forced a change in the college constitution (Lindinger, 1991, p. 11). In response, Aicher took over as rector in 1962, sought balance between theory and practice, and redefined the primary mission of the design curriculum as one of practical not theoretical development. The Basic Course was replaced by first-year study in one of the four departments.

Ulm Product Design projects went beyond the Bauhaus interest in furnishings and included highly utilitarian objects—a handheld drill, fountain pen, residential sanitation system—that were more typically the work of engineers, not designers. Rittel argued that, "The designer complements the work of the engineer, architect, or scientist . . . and also controls an important area of no-man's-land between all these specialties" (Lindinger, 1991, p. 94). Even when designing furniture, Hans Gugelot's studios worked in seating systems rather than the design of individual chairs. The school built strong collaborations with Braun, Lufthansa, and Kodak and addressed the issues of mass production and technology in guiding the work of the studios.

The Visual Communication studios addressed typography, graphic design, photography, exhibition design, and packaging, with attention to the problems of advertising. Early visual studies included systematic investigations of graph configurations and typographic systems that avoided the early modernist use of lines and graphic elements to separate units of information, believing the intent of those devices was to overcome insufficient coding of typographic form. Later curricular components included the study of sign systems under Maldonado, Aicher, and Guy Bonsiepe, who went on to become an interface designer. This interest in systems was consistently integrated with the school's social agenda, in contrast to a more reductivist goal of producing visual similarity among elements.

A curriculum document from the first years of the program identified visual communication research as "fitting visual statements as closely as possible to what they have to say" (1958–1959 HfG curriculum document, as cited in Lindinger, 1991, p. 141). Ulm faculty supported the belief that the more designers concentrated on the aesthetics of form, the more their social and political complicity with the communications industry could be concealed (Lindinger, 1991). Following the outcomes of German rhetoric during the war years, Ulm advocated transparency in communication at all costs.

Originally conceived by Bill as a public relations department, the Information curriculum was developed under scientist Max Bense. It looked at texts in terms of the quantity and complexity of information they contained through a systematic approach based on information theory. Applications in journalism drove projects; however, students also explored scientific texts and criticism as well. Literature on the program likened the Ulm environment to the Bauhaus after World War II but distanced itself in its response. The goal was described as bringing "cells of order to the world," recalling the rhetorical dangers exemplified by Hitler's propaganda machine (Gert Kalow 1957–1958, as cited in Lindinger, 1991, p. 172). Under-enrolled, the program eventually merged with Visual Communications.

Although there was no traditional architecture program at Ulm, the Building program addressed problems presented by the industrialization of construction. It embodied concern for structural changes within the organizations that proposed and constructed buildings; the mechanization of construction techniques; new building materials; and research (Lindinger, 1991). Instruction in drawing and urban planning presumed prior architectural training for students admitted to the program. The curriculum was decidedly utopian in its approach. Faculty envisioned designing a new society and meeting mass needs. Study included the human sciences and areas previously the concern of engineers. It emphasized a modular approach to architecture based on lightweight geometric forms that could be recombined in different building types, another iteration of the institution's interest in systems. The program conducted experiments on new cladding and window systems and the application of new industrial processes and materials in construction. Faculty deliberately avoided the term "architecture" in favor of "building" as more comprehensive (Lindinger, 1991).

By 1968 the financial structure for the school was no longer viable: a number of courses were cancelled, faculty were let go, and the institution's debts were mounting. There were government talks of a merger with the Ulm School of Engineering, and faculty continued to argue over curriculum. Students protested over the relevance of curricula in light of newer, more radical ideas about design and renounced the curriculum in a 1968 open letter to the faculty. British design historian Reyner Banham argued that designers should take seriously the American interest in style, a challenge to the problem-solving orientation of Ulm (Aynsley, 2009). Ultimately, the Regional Parliament withdrew its funding, closing the school at the same time that others around the world reassessed the benefits of modernism.

Ironically, the strongest reputation of the Ulm School of Design now stems from its style, a clean look and attention to industrial production that often concealed its social agenda. Students in the later years of the school lamented that Ulm products for Braun filled catalogs, side by side with an array of unremarkable objects, and that the importance of Ulm's social agenda was lost on both industry and consumers (Aynsley, 2009).

In fact, Ulm made important contributions to design education and professional practice that are often overshadowed by the better-known and more popular pedagogical strategies of the Bauhaus. Ulm's role in expanding study beyond art and design influenced many of today's university curricula. In particular, Ulm established relevance in the study of science and theory. Today's programs in building science owe much to the concerns of faculty at Ulm, and the institution's integration of ergonomics, engineering, and human sciences are now accepted components of most industrial design curricula. The kinds of problems tackled in the Ulm studios also encouraged collaboration across fields and eventual interest by other disciplines in design. Ways of working in Ulm set the stage for today's design responses to complex social and technological challenges.

The introduction of semiotics transformed communication design curricula. There are few programs today that don't teach some aspect of linguistic theories as fundamental to the study of visual messages, although Rhode Island School of Design—under Dutch designers Thomas Ockerse and Hans van Dijk—pioneered the application of semiotic theories for American schools of design. Although writing currently remains on the periphery of many communication design curricula, there are a number of programs that devote significant attention to rhetoric, consistent with the emphasis of Ulm's short-lived Information department.

Ulm also led work in design research, planning, and methods. Bruce Archer—who joined the Ulm faculty at the request of Tomas Maldonado—left the school to establish the Design Research program at the Royal College of Art in London and to publish on issues of design research throughout his lengthy career. Although work at Ulm was more speculation than rigorously constructed scientific experiment, the attention to methods and frequent borrowing of principles from more established fields of study signaled an interest in the consequences of design action. In the 1960s and 1970s, an interest in methods spread and resulted in books such as *Design Methods* by J. Christopher Jones and *Problem Seeking* by William Peña. Suited to the complexity of problems in postindustrial society, this focus on design methods grew beyond schools of design to spawn a plethora of contemporary books in business, technology, and education. And more recently, schools have developed methods-centered graduate programs, such as the Master of Design Methods at the Institute of Design/Illinois Institute of Technology and the study of transition design at Carnegie Mellon University.

Ulm also focused designers' attention on systems thinking as necessary to work on complex problems. The primary concerns were not the appearance of related objects or graphic components but the interdependencies and forces that govern the behavior of large-scale social, cultural, physical, and technological structures. This attitude would become increasingly important in twenty-first-century practice as design problems shifted from artifacts to tools and systems.

REJECTING THE MODERNIST PARADIGM

In the last decades of the twentieth century, two forces converged in an assault on the modernist paradigm: digital technology and postmodern critical theory. Both fostered a period of experimentation that challenged ideas of universal form, objectivity, and social progress through art and design. In many cases, the implications of this new focus first found support in schools of design, rather than professional practice.

The development of digital technology and design software opened opportunities for the liberation of form from the minimalist vocabulary of modernism and freedom from the constraints of traditional production and editorial processes. Students could design and produce new forms with extreme precision and combine imagery in ways not possible under traditional methods, thus expanding the visual repertoire of design beyond the rational geometry of mid-twentieth-century work. At the same time that digital technology concealed the "hand" of the individual designer and traces of industrial-age production, it allowed young designers to repurpose the "low art" of found, vernacular forms and ad hoc technologies that their modernist predecessors discounted as unharmonious and unsuitable for elevating culture. And students could produce and publish finished-looking work without the approval of editors and sponsorship of clients, circulating their experiments beyond the limits of their classrooms.

This shift in form and its underlying challenges to long-standing modernist principles were not broadly understood. In an *Eye* magazine article titled "Cult of the Ugly," graphic design historian Steven Heller described a cross-institutional graduate student publication, *Output*, as "leaving the reader confused as to its purpose and another 'experiment' in the current plethora of aesthetically questionable graphic output . . . ugliness in the service of fashionable experimentation" (Heller, 1993). Yale graphic design faculty Michael Rock commented in the *AIGA Journal*, "That contemporary design education has been thrown into a state of confusion both aggravates and reflects a pervasive professional confusion. It is inherently impractical to fully prepare students to work in a field that has so little sense of its immediate future or professional position" (Rock, 1995, p. 12).

California Institute of the Arts professor Lorraine Wild published a seminal text in the early 1990s, titled *On Overcoming Modernism*, which countered the notion that practice and education had temporarily lost consensus about what constitutes "good design" through an argument that symptoms of a radically different postmodernity constituted a new context for practice:

> In recent years universality has collapsed into multi-culturalism, focus groups, zip-code clusters, etc.; objectivity has collapsed into subjectivity, at the same time as the author and subject, or both, have been declared dead in some quarters; and the optimistic march of progress has been cancelled. The linear is harder to detect and the simultaneous has become habitual (Wild, 1994, p. 56).

Supporting postmodern ideas of culture as inherently pluralistic and built over time, the study of design history and criticism gained a new foothold in American design schools. By the mid-1970s, MIT, Cornell, Columbia, Berkeley, and Princeton had PhD programs in architectural history as offerings distinct from art history. There were concurrent efforts to publish the first comprehensive histories of graphic and industrial design, not as sidebars to major art movements but as freestanding chronologies that supported new accreditation requirements to teach the history of the design disciplines. In many cases, studio faculty—Philip Meggs, Ellen Lupton, Doug Scott, Arthur Pulos, Roger Remington, Andrew Blauvelt, Martha Scotford, and Lorraine Wild, for example—authored early discussions of design history, filling the scholarship and teaching gap created by American art historians. Even today, studio faculty deliver a disproportionate percentage of instruction in graphic and industrial design history in American colleges and universities, and unlike architecture, it is still difficult to find doctoral programs dedicated to the history of these subjects in the United States. Alternative historical perspectives also emerged, often based on political, technological, and economic change, rather than the traditional art historical canon of famous people and the objects they made.

Important writing in philosophy and cultural theory—by Roland Barthes, Michel Foucault, Jean Baudrillard, Jacques Derrida, Martin Heidegger, Jürgen Habermas, and others—in the last half of the twentieth century also stimulated discourse regarding the continuing relevance of modernist ideas in design. Architect Robert Venturi delivered a paper titled *Complexity and Contradiction in Architecture* at the Museum of Modern Art in 1966. His gentle manifesto celebrated elements that were "hybrid, rather than pure," and advocated "a messy vitality over an obvious unity . . . richness of meaning rather than clarity of meaning" in architecture (Venturi, 1966, p. 16). In *Learning from*

Las Vegas, he called for architects to be more open to the tastes of common people and less concerned with self-referential monuments. Not long after Venturi's speech, architectural critic Charles Jencks published *The Language of Post-Modern Architecture* and lectured in architecture schools around the world about work that derived its nature from context and cultural symbols, not purely from function and structure.

In many cases, however, graduate students led the way in unseating the dominant modernist ideology in design. Master's students at Cranbrook Academy of Art, under the mentorship of Michael and Katherine McCoy, explored the product and communication design implications of European postmodern texts, citing the inevitability of the designer having a cultural position, the responsibility of the reader in constructing meaning, and the pluralism of colliding cultural signifiers in postindustrial society. In *Cranbrook Design: The New Discourse*, Katherine McCoy wrote:

"Correct" form and the univalent "universal" criteria of Modernism are often rejected, reflecting the pluralistic cultural fragmentation of our post-Modern, post industrial milieu. The look and structure of graphic form is underplayed in favor of verbal signification, valuing semantic expression over syntactical style. Cranbrook graphic work has moved from lyrical celebration of form to a critical discourse on the meaning of form (McCoy, 1990, p. 17).

During this period, the graduate graphic design program at Rhode Island School of Design began a long teaching relationship with Dutch design educator Jan van Toorn. Semiotics was a well-established interest in the RISD curriculum and provided a platform for new studies of the role of form in the construction of meaning. Van Toorn encouraged graduate students to develop a practice that reflected on the designer's dialogic relationship with the reader. He challenged designers to counteract the modernist use of symbols by revealing the relationship between political, social, and economic power structures and readers' interpretations—a subversive "outing" of the designer's manipulation, achieved through images that were intentionally provocative and ambiguous in their meaning.

Sheila Levrant de Bretteville inherited the forty-year modernist tradition of Yale University when she became the director of graphic design studies in 1990. A devout feminist, De Bretteville quickly refocused the program on the individual differences between designers and their audiences. She built a curriculum that challenged the modernist view of one reader or audience through broad exposure to a variety of critical perspectives, often from outside the field of design. She sent students out into the community for engagement with audiences around important issues, a "relational existence" that deals with contradictions and questions, rather than answers. It is not surprising that de Bretteville's populist agenda found inspiration in the writings of architect Venturi.

Graduates of these early programs went on to teach at other schools and into practice with stylistic approaches to cultural projects that offered alternatives to the modernist form favored by corporate America. Cranbrook alumna Lorraine Wild reflected in a 2000 interview with *Eye* magazine.

> . . . the academic visual experiments of the late 1980s and early 1990s took the path (how could they not?) of moving first from the connection to that profound questioning of design, and then to being understood as a symbol of that questioning, and then to being accepted as an "alternative" style, and then finally to mass commercial usage, which of course has led to its stylistic demise . . . At CalArts in the mid-1990s we watched our students emulate the postmodern stylistic trajectory. It was then we knew it was time, not only to question the style, but to incorporate—in the teaching of typography, for instance—a reconsideration of the historical development of visuality as a vehicle for understanding design (Wild & Sandhaus, 2000).

Although postmodern stylistic explorations waned in the face of more pressing issues in the professions—including rapidly evolving networked technology, concern for sustainable practices, and increased accountability for predicting the outcomes of design action—this stream of theoretical inquiry in American architecture and design schools produced greater distinction between undergraduate and graduate education. In programs where postmodern ideas were supported by deep reading and discourse, curricula were distinctly different from the general preparation for employment of most undergraduate programs. And a small collection of schools established themselves as centers for study under particular philosophies, helping students to make clear decisions about where to do graduate work that was consistent with their interests.

THE CONTEMPORARY CONTEXT FOR DESIGN EDUCATION

For most of the twentieth century, the primary role of design was to make things look and work better, to support the functional and emotional experiences of consumers through well-designed artifacts and places. Design controlled the physical attributes of communication, objects, and environments and assigned high priority to craftsmanship, originality, and individual authorship. These values shaped design education, rewarding students for the novelty of their solutions and mastery of materials and technologies. Faculty typically scaffolded curricular experiences from simple to complex, starting with exercises that established a vocabulary of form and moving toward consideration of audience or users and context later in the curriculum. As new skills and content emerged, faculty added them to the course of study in upper-level offerings but rarely rethought the relevance of beginning instruction under new paradigms for practice.

Today, the expanded role of networked technology in our everyday lives, growing participation by users in the generation of form and content, and increasing interdependency among complex social, economic, and physical systems call into question the efficacy of traditional approaches to framing and solving problems in design education as well as practice. Donald Norman—author of *The Design of Everyday Things*, former vice president of Apple's Advanced Technology Group, and director of the University of California/ San Diego Design Lab—lists five major principles of twentieth-century design that are no longer suited to contemporary design problems:

- Linear causal relationships underpin assumptions that a preferred state can be achieved by design fixing a root cause of friction;
- Narrowly defined contexts as problem settings suggest the engagement of relatively few disciplines;
- Independent elements can be addressed one at a time without throwing an entire system out of balance;
- Operating constraints as stable and recurring; and
- Relatively few mutually incompatible constraints make it likely that competing priorities can be resolved to some degree of satisfaction (Norman & Stappers, 2016, p. 1).

The point Norman makes is that complex problems in the contemporary context for design involve perpetually changing relationships among countless interdependent variables, making it impossible to address one variable at a time in isolation or through a single discipline (Davis, 2016). Artifact-driven strategies fall short in addressing problems at this scale, yet most of today's design education is structured in terms of defining the physical attributes of discrete objects and environments, not in terms of interacting systems.

Designer Hugh Dubberly describes two types of design practice that emerged over the last two decades. Design for interaction changed the focus of practice from artifacts to simulations, stories, and tools through which people create their own experiences. In 1998—under the leadership of designer Clement Mok—the AIGA convened a group of forty designers, design educators, and technologists to define emerging principles for the new medium of experience design. There was tension within the group over whether this new practice was an extension of traditional communication design in a new medium or an opportunity to establish entirely new relationships between designers and the people who benefit from their work. Because discussion preceded bursting of the dot. com bubble in 2001, most participants thought in terms of buying-and-selling transactions. It was a small group of educators who admonished the group to think about consequences of the practice for learning, leisure, work, and participation in the privileges of democracy.

Among those with greater hopes for the medium, Dubberly interviewed early developers of interaction design about their processes. Their approaches to problems were significantly different from those of artifact-oriented practices. With the goals of shaping behavior, designing systems with feedback loops, and facilitating active engagement with information as content producers as well as users, today's interaction design practices routinely include user-centered research, development of personas and scenarios, and rapid prototyping and integrated systems for user feedback (Dubberly, 2005). It is understood that the stopping condition is "good enough for now"—not "almost perfect," as in artifact-oriented work—because technological systems evolve (Dubberly, 2005).

Design education responded to this paradigm shift in different ways. While some programs recognized the challenges interaction design posed to conventional curricular and pedagogical strategies—building new course sequences that introduced students to systems and user-centered research in their earliest design classes—others simply added interaction design courses to the upper levels of conventional curricula with few changes in preparatory study. In many programs, student work took on "the look of interaction" (buttons, rollovers, and scrolling), rather than deeper attempts to align the user's perception of the informational and technical systems with their actual behavior. Other programs gravitated toward "motion graphics" and "game design" as commercial applications that brought movement and user engagement to traditional storytelling. Graphic and industrial design programs that resisted work in interactive and networked technology altogether often found themselves competing side by side with "new media" programs for talented students.

Dubberly also identifies a second emerging practice as design for conversation. Unlike the asymmetrical relationships of interaction design in which users simply respond to commands from designed systems, conversation design engages users as co-creators who contribute both content and form to the design of services, platforms, and communities of interest.

The design of service ecologies constitutes increasing percentages of professional design work. The US Bureau of Labor Statistics predicts the majority of growth in the US economy will be in service-providing sectors over the next five years. Zipcar makes nothing but provides user access to a fleet of 12,000 cars in eight countries. Apple built its successful customer service strategy in stores—where T-shirted clerks greet and triage customers' needs upon entry—on the model of concierge services in luxury hotels. Design consultancy Fjord describes the new service design challenges of the future. "Managing the gaps in consumer experience between the physical and digital channels and across services, devices, and places . . . reducing the pain of navigating an experience fragmented by specialized services and applications" will define new online experiences (Fjord, 2015). The task for designers is to bridge experiences separated by time, place, and sponsor.

Platforms are technological systems that support the design of applications and technologies by third parties. The Apple app store now contains more than 1.5 million applications, most of them built by others on the Apple platform. Google, Facebook, Microsoft, and Amazon are also in the platform business. These systems control the kinds of communication that are possible. Engagement of designers in this type of work requires an education that is not about the use of software but about working in interdisciplinary teams to determine new technological affordances and interfaces and applications that may not even be visual.

Dubberly describes the design of communities as negotiating the rules and frameworks that govern interactions among participants with provision for changing rules as the community evolves. Whether physical or virtual, the task is not the arrangement of form but creating the potential for particular kinds of experiences. Dubberly's firm, for example, reimagined National Geographic as a membership organization that returned to its nineteenth-century roots as a group interested in expeditions. The proposal allowed citizen scientists to feed information to the organization, to interact with photographers in the field, and to extend the resources of explorers in classrooms.

Design work at this scale requires research. Rick Robinson, applied researcher in material and cultural studies and founder of the design research firm Iota Partners (now Sapient), says, "By advocating that design be considered a strategic voice in product development, communications, and marketing, the field has been asked to play by the same rules and be measured by the same yardstick as other principal business activities . . . Research needs to be justified on an ongoing, long-term basis, not purely on a 'see what we found!' case-by-case basis" (Robinson, 2016; Davis, 2016). Robinson describes off-the-shelf technologies—smartphones and sensor-based devices, such as the Nest thermostat that detects residents' movement in homes—as useful in a data-aware effort to understand human behavior. Designers need to develop skills in mining this data for meaningful patterns that inform design decisions, for making sense of what Robinson calls the "faces, places, and traces" of digital activity.

A design education that responds to this radically changed environment and scale of activity will not arise from the logical progression of artifact-based curricula and pedagogies. Neither is it likely that defining graduate education as the refinement of undergraduate skills will produce professional leaders and faculty who can shape the future of these practices. Clearly, it is time for a new educational paradigm that in many respects breaks the lineage from early craft guilds and drawing schools, while maintaining the focus on intellectual flexibility and concern for human values that are characteristic of the earliest design practices. It is in this spirit that the following chapters lay the groundwork for shaping new design curricula.

CHAPTER 2:
DESIGNING EFFECTIVE CURRICULA

Years ago, I met with the president of a well-known college of art and design who was searching for a provost. His background was in arts management, but our conversation eventually came around to the course of study at the college. When asked about curriculum, he said, "Curriculum, yes! I need one of those!"

We all need one of those! The relationship between institutions and students is contractual. Students enroll in a college or university program with the expectation that the content of their design education will be relevant at the time they graduate. More important, the institution has an obligation to ensure that the lasting content of the discipline and approaches to lifelong learning balance training and skills that are temporarily marketable.

Institutions need a systematic way of fulfilling this contract. Curriculum is an educated "best guess" by faculty regarding the knowledge, skills, and perspectives that will define both the intellectual discipline of design and professional competency for years to come. Curricular decisions determine the entry employment qualifications of new practitioners but also beginning designers' abilities to evolve as professionals and informed citizens across careers that last fifty years or more.

I recently delivered a convocation speech to students and faculty at the start of their academic year. My tenure in the College of Design at North Carolina State University comprised the second half of my professional life, making it a convenient period of time for comparing my previous work in design practice with current conditions in the field. I described more than a decade of running a design office by showing slides of the first cordless phone; bike messengers who carried comprehensive layouts from the design office to clients; typewritten manuscripts marked up with specifications for phototypesetters; mechanical boards for the delivery of camera-ready art to printers; and the firm's first computer, an Apple 2c (256K memory), which required yards of hexadecimal code to move simple geometric shapes across the screen in one color.

I then listed changes in technology over the last twenty-six years (Figure 2.1). My point for students and faculty was that nothing about the skills-based training of my design education prepared me for a world completely

FIGURE 2.1 *Changes in communication technology.*

1988	First truly portable digital camera
1990	Recordable CDs
1991	Source code released for the world wide web
1991	Mosaic web browser
1993	Digital printing
1993	Email (average use in 2012=13 hours per week)
1995	Amazon.com goes online
1996	GPS available to the public
1996	*New York Times* goes online
1997	Google domain name registered
2000	Dot-com bubble bursts
2001	Apple iPod and iTunes
2001	Wikipedia launches (17M articles, 262 languages)
2002	IBM stops making computers
2003	Adobe Creative Suite
2004	Facebook (used by 1/3 of US citizens in 2015)
2004	Flickr (Pinterest launches in 2010)
2005	Youtube's first video uploaded ("Me at the Zoo")
2006	Skype for Mac (500M installs in 2015)
2007	Apple iPhone
2008	Apple Store (1.6 million 3rd party apps in 2015)
2007	Kindle e-book reader (3.6M books in 2015)
2008	Spotify launches
2010	Apple iPad
2010	Instagram
2010	DIY 3-D printers commercially available
2012	Kodak and Fuji stop making film
2013	Google Glass beta tested
2014	Nintendo sales reach 670M hardware units
2015	Apple Watch ships to customers
2015	Microsoft Windows Holographic announced

reconfigured by digital technology. My ability to adapt to a professional environment of complex, systems-level problems, rapid technological change, increasing participation by users in the design process, and greater accountability for predicting the outcomes of design action had little to do with technical skills or even with the invention of visual form. This discussion was not to diminish the importance of skills or to devalue the role of creative work, but simply to say that a curriculum designed for the moment and approaches to learning that focus only on technique are likely to fall short across a professional lifetime. The content of an educational experience needs to ensure that students grasp the concepts at the heart of the discipline and the overarching content of a strong general education in order to make sense of more profound changes in the culture at large.

CURRICULUM AND ENDURING CONTENT

Grant Wiggins and Jay McTighe, in *Understanding by Design*, address three types of content knowledge that make up curricula. First, there are the things with which students should be familiar—to have seen, read, heard, or otherwise encountered (Wiggins and McTighe, 1998). In college-level design programs, this type of content knowledge might include specific visual examples, designers' names, and dates from design history; critical essays and articles on recent practice; or current terminology used by professionals in their work. Such knowledge is usually temporary in its relevance. Specific names and dates aren't the real meaning of history but are useful as references in class assignments and as entry points to understanding larger concepts. The specific topics of many essays or presentations fade in importance over time, but they serve as provocative prompts in learning how to talk critically about design. And relevant terminology changes as practice and culture evolve. Faculty can assess this type of familiar knowledge through conversation, writing, and pencil-and-paper tests.

The authors describe the second type of content knowledge as theories and skills related to the discipline and practice (Wiggins and McTighe, 1998). Particular perspectives on the role of social media, drawing, and methods for integrating design in business are likely to be useful longer than content in the first category of knowledge, but their significance in the discipline and practice eventually wanes over time. Theories go out of fashion—I no longer assign postmodern critical theorist Jacques Derrida as reading for my graduate students—and changes in the surrounding context for practice require new explanations of how design and business work together. While many faculty argue that drawing will always be important to design, its applications change under new technologies, and there are successful designers who never draw in today's practices. Although faculty can assess some theoretical content knowledge through writing and discussions with students, they best understand students' mastery of skills through performance in task-oriented assignments.

Knowledge that is at the core of the discipline and likely to define practice over time comprises Wiggins and McTighe's third type of curricular content (Wiggins and McTighe, 1998). While skill in using a particular software program is temporarily relevant knowledge, criticality in making choices among ways of producing something is not. Designers may not use specific examples from design history across their careers, but understanding how social, cultural, technological, and economic conditions led to particular design responses is insight that informs contemporary decision-making. The ways through which faculty teach even the transitory content of the field and entry-level skills demanded by employers, therefore, can determine whether students view such knowledge only as instrumental in meeting curricular requirements and getting a job, or as opportunities linked to larger concepts and perspectives that are likely to persist.

Faculty assess enduring understanding through performance—through critical judgments made throughout the design process, not through tests. Wiggins and McTighe describe aspects of understanding that constitute hierarchical and observable evidence of mastery: explanation, interpretation, application, holding a perspective, empathy, and self-knowledge (Wiggins & McTighe, 1998). Students may be able to *explain* something, for example, but not *interpret* its significance. *Application* requires deep understanding of concepts in contexts other than the one through which faculty initially introduced them. *Holding a perspective* on design depends on curricular experiences that address alternate views of the discipline and practice. Mature students *empathize* not only with users but also with classmates and collaborators who have opinions other than their own. And students operating at the upper levels of understanding *know what they don't know*—they function metacognitively and regulate their own behavior throughout the learning process, especially after failure. These aspects of understanding are useful in developing learning outcomes (because they describe observable behaviors) and in assessing

student performance (because they represent a continuum of developing abilities). Later discussions in this book address these issues.

The challenge for faculty in designing curriculum, therefore, is to determine the appropriate distribution of these types of content knowledge across
a course of study that serves the mission of the degree program. There is
external pressure by institutional administrators and employers to focus on the
first two types of knowledge—things to be familiar with and skills—because
measurement appears objective and the connection to entry-level employment is obvious. But programs have limited time with students. Emphasis on
one type of knowledge is always at the expense of another. Because design is a
rapidly evolving field, faculty must anticipate the lifespan of different kinds of
knowledge. Too much time devoted to content that is temporarily significant
means that students graduate unprepared for decades-long careers.

Curriculum Development Is a Design Problem

Faculty design curricula, just as practitioners design solutions to clients' problems. Developing a course of study requires analyzing contexts and stakeholders, articulating priorities and desired outcomes, generating alternatives,
prototyping solutions, and evaluating short- and long-term consequences. It
is puzzling that faculty highly skilled in design often default to their own educational experiences as curricular templates for a new institution, even when
their students and context are radically different from the original setting.
Other faculty simply ignore the larger structure that organizes educational
experiences for students, focusing instead on their own courses. Curricula in
these programs are often a cafeteria of "cult of personality" offerings from
which students must build independent but rarely challenged understanding of
the discipline and practice. It says something about curriculum design when a
student's answer to the question, "What courses are you taking this semester?"
is "Bailey, Smith, and Jones," rather than a description of design content.

Like the practice of design, curriculum development involves cycles of
projection, planning, implementation, and *evaluation* (Figure 2. 2). Design programs
frequently plan and implement but rarely project and evaluate systematically or
in depth. This shortfall is of some concern to the field as increasing numbers of
young faculty enter teaching without deep backgrounds in design practice that
shape their understanding of a rapidly changing field. They often base curriculum design on limited firsthand knowledge or traditional models for structuring

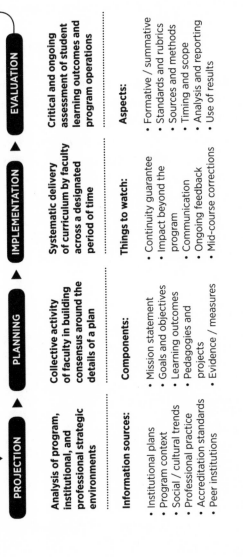

FIGURE 2.2 *The above chart explains the curriculum design process and issues related to each stage. Typically, faculty plan and implement but rarely project and evaluate in systematic ways. As a result, curriculum becomes insular, a mismatch with the forces that define the contemporary context for design practice and education.*

the course of study. Further, many faculty believe that the criteria for evaluating curricular performance in design fall outside the standardized metrics of the institution and view the formal assessment task as irrelevant in day-to-day instruction. This perception suggests that design programs may lack convincing evidence through which a counting-and-measuring culture rewards success.

PROJECTING FUTURE CONDITIONS

Curriculum is a response to the strategic environment for design practice and education; a proposition for how to meet the demands on learning presented by problems in the profession and society. Curriculum can react to the current state of things, or it can anticipate emerging challenges in this environment. Anticipatory design programs study trends, evaluate their significance, and predict their trajectories.

There are several sources of information that inform projections and planning in a strategic environment for design education and practice:

- Institutional strategic plans
- Institutional context
- Social and cultural trends
- Design practice
- Accreditation standards
- Peer institutions

Institutional Strategic Plans

Typically, institutions acknowledge trends that influence education, research, and professional work for their graduates through strategic plans. Such plans guide decisions, policies, and incentives for academic programs and faculty. Design education programs that monitor and make decisions in recognition of these larger priorities generally do better in securing new resources and achieving recognition within their institutions than programs with independent agendas.

For example, if the institution describes expanding its global presence as a strategic goal, then administration may show greater interest in developing study abroad programs than in other proposals for curricular expansion. Likewise, the influence of design alumni on international practice may be important to document when reporting to administration. If the institutional goal is to improve student retention, then programs that focus on policies and academic support for first-year students are more likely to fair well in evaluations than programs that cross their fingers and hope that enrollment patterns stabilize. Programs frequently have greater success when curricular planning and resource requests align with institutional priorities, yet art and design faculty often ignore strategic plans as irrelevant to their program agendas. It is important to demonstrate to administration how the design program is essential to achieving the institution's goals, not special and outside overall standards for evaluating effectiveness. Special is often the first thing to go when an institution considers what it can and cannot afford.

Institutional Context

The mission of an institution and the location of the program within a particular academic unit usually guide decisions regarding possible purposes for design curricula. Multipurpose universities, for example, offer a wide array of nondesign courses, diverse faculty resources, and comprehensive library collections that may not be present in an independent school of art and design. These resources support a broad inventory of curricular perspectives and collaborative opportunities with other disciplines, as well as development of students' research skills. The presence of mature research disciplines on campus also sets the standards for the evaluation of design faculty and expectations for how scholarship informs teaching.

Independent schools of art and design in cities with established professional design cultures frequently rely on part-time instructors from practice. Part-time faculty, however, rarely participate in the detailed work of curriculum development, management, and assessment, so specific procedures need to be in place to make good use of practical knowledge and to ensure continuity in students' curricular experiences across courses. Art and design schools also streamline procedures for curriculum approval and often rely on professional staff rather than faculty for recruitment and advising. In some cases, this means greater autonomy from protracted approval processes for implementing new courses.

University communication, industrial, and interior design programs often reside in departments or colleges of fine art, although more recently some have migrated to colleges of design and/or architecture. Other design curricula can be found in mass communication, business, engineering, environmental studies, or the humanities. Location determines the ideological perspectives, pedagogical practices, and standards for evaluation in the surrounding culture. It influences who applies for admission and students' expectations of academic life during enrollment and after graduation. Location also guides faculty hires, typical work-loads, and the nature of scholarship. It is common for design programs to have the largest student enrollment in a department or college but to be ideologically very different from other fields in the same academic unit. This situation creates challenges and opportunities as faculty negotiate admissions priorities, common courses for all majors, and professional opportunities for students.

I first taught communication design in a university school of art with painters and sculptors, and later in a university school of design with architects and industrial designers. Students' admission to the common first-year pro-gram in the school of art required adequate academic credentials and a strong response to thirteen visual assignments. Department faculty re-reviewed stu-dents' portfolios after completion of freshmen studios for admission to the communication design major. The general education requirements of the university were minimal, and writing and art history were taught in sections comprised entirely of art and design majors.

Admission to the school of design was directly into the communica-tion design major, although students in all design disciplines had a common first semester of design study. Admission procedures first required very high academic qualifications, followed by a review of portfolios and essays, and finally interviews with faculty. Design majors had the highest academic pro-files of any freshmen cohort entering the university, and general education requirements were very demanding (for example, two required semesters of college-level calculus).

The studio credits in these two programs were roughly the same—both curricula met the requirements for the professional degree—but the stu-dents were differently talented. Art school students were generally intuitive and technically proficient but needed a heavy hand from faculty in learn-ing to organize investigations, address user-centered issues, and reach closure on projects. Design school students were hyperorganized and good at anal-ysis but had to be weaned from faculty assurance that a plan would produce good results before proceeding with risky ideas. Both schools produced good designers but the approaches to curriculum and instruction that served these two student profiles needed to be quite different.

Projections of the strategic environment for design study should also acknowledge other opportunities within the institutional context, such as research centers and related curricular programs that are likely collaborators. Many nonvisual disciplines show great interest in design, and institutions value faculty and students working across disciplines. Studies indicate that faculty relationships, not administrative mandates, lay the strongest foundations for interdisciplinary partnerships (NC State University, 2011). At the same time, these relationships require administrative support in eliminating barriers, such as formulas for faculty workloads and credit-hour production, cost sharing, scheduling, and evaluation of collaborative work in tenure and promotion decisions.

Social and Cultural Trends

Design is a social practice. It both illustrates and shapes culture. Any significant change in the surrounding culture places new demands on designers to respond. Design faculty don't have to be experts in determining trends that are likely to have influence. There are people who do this for a living.

Management consultants at McKinsey, for example, produce reports on topics ranging from technology trends to global competition. Fjord, a design innovation company, publishes discussions of new opportunities—on issues of youth engagement, wearable technologies, and service design, for example—and an annual trends report. Faculty in business and the social sciences examine shifts in the nature of work. Roger Martin at the Prosperity Institute at the University of Toronto, for example, publishes detailed analyses of patterns in work with specific implications for design practice. His colleague, Richard Florida, follows trends in creative production, describing the character and location of centers of innovation. And professional design associations frequently convene leaders in the field to assess how conditions might change as a way of framing programming for its members.

The public sector also tracks educational trends. The US government forms blue-ribbon panels to articulate challenges ahead for education and business. For example, the Department of Labor *Secretary's Commission on Achieving Necessary Skills* (SCANS) report described the demands that work places on education in the twenty-first century. The Knowledgeworks Foundation follows trends in education and culture, predicting issues that will affect the future of learning. The MacArthur Foundation and the Organization for

Economic Cooperation and Development (OECD) studied the use of technology in the classroom. More recently, the OECD convened an international panel to articulate proficiency levels in college students' acquisition of innovation skills, with particular attention to the use of design thinking as a pedagogical strategy.

Watching and reading about these trends informs faculty's curricular planning. Faculty must make decisions about the significance of a trend in design and its sphere of influence, but there is good information available about cultural change to supplement faculty's general impressions of forces affecting design practice.

Design Practice

There is much to learn from design professionals, including alumni, practitioners who teach, and cutting-edge design offices that are leading changes in the field. Many academic programs maintain external advisory boards to stay informed of shifts in the models of practice. It is important to choose advisors for their diversity of opinion and experience, not primarily for their familiarity with the program and its faculty. Alumni, for example, often reinforce the traditional orientation of their alma mater and may represent a narrow slice of practice or a particular geographic region. Good advisors challenge the status quo and ask hard questions about curricular relevancy. And it is also important to structure mechanisms for their input, informing them fully of the state of the program and asking for meaningful response through a well-articulated agenda.

While faculty can gain valuable curricular recommendations through personal contact with individual practitioners, it is also important to monitor discourse among the most forward-thinking professionals in the field. Social anthropologist Jean Lave and learning theorist Etienne Wenger wrote in the 1990s about "communities of practice." They described learning as something we do not only individually when in school but also throughout our lives in social contact with people who have common concerns. These communities are not just special interest groups whose members devote attention to the same subject matter, but people who build meaningful relationships through which they learn about professional practice from each other. They share experiences, ways of thinking about the work they do, and a network of connections that distinguish them from others (Lave and Wenger, 1991; Davis, 2016).

Studying the discourse within and among communities of practice is especially relevant to projection in a field that changes as rapidly as design. Communities of practice are more agile in responding to new conditions than are formal institutions or established fields of study. Their ideas are critiqued on the basis of actual performance and are rarely confined by disciplinary or organizational boundaries. It is possible, therefore, to understand an evolving profession by studying discourse in its communities of practice. Members frequently summarize discussions in manifestos, opinion editorials in publications, anthologies on particular topics, and conference presentations and proceedings (Davis, 2016).

Accreditation Standards

Most institutions in the United States hold accreditation under their respective regional agencies. Many art and design programs seek additional disciplinary accreditation from organizations such as: the National Association of Schools of Art and Design (NASAD); Council of Interior Design Accreditation (CIDA); and National Architectural Accrediting Board (NAAB). These agencies publish standards of operation and student competencies for which member schools are accountable. In some cases, as in architecture, disciplinary accreditation is required for graduates of programs to qualify for licensure. In other cases, disciplinary accreditation is optional. All agencies evaluate programs through peer-review processes at regular intervals. Programs that seek accreditation study standards when planning and evaluating curricula and many coordinate accreditation reports and reviews with required institutional assessments to avoid duplicate efforts. Review by peer members provides external assessment of curricula against national benchmarks, which strengthens the case for curricula within institutions and assures prospective students that a course of study produces advertised outcomes.

It is common, however, for programs to misinterpret accreditation standards as requiring a discrete course for each student competency. Without exception, accrediting agencies describe what students should know and be able to do, not the curricular organization or pedagogical practices through which programs produce such outcomes. Several accrediting agencies offer consultants and workshops for administrators in preparation for accreditation and are especially helpful when faculty are considering major changes to their degree offerings.

Regardless of an institution's choice about disciplinary accreditation, external review of curricula should be a consistent practice for ensuring that faculty perceptions are consistent with best practices in the field.

Peer Institutions

How peers address the strategic environment for design and design education can be helpful in curriculum development. Many institutions have a peer list they use for benchmarking purposes; however, these are often not peers in design. It is useful for design programs to observe and maintain contact with faculty from two types of institutions: peer programs that are contextually or structurally similar and peer programs that are successful at something design faculty aspire to, regardless of how the institution is organized.

Programs that share an institutional context can reveal something about the intellectual and strategic resources necessary to support curricular practices. For example, the curricular possibilities for a program located in a small liberal arts college may be very different from those of a large public university with a technology focus. The standards and procedures for establishing new graduate programs in a research university may be very different from those of a single discipline art school that has a limited history of offering advanced study. Programs with similar organizational structures for decision-making can offer insights on planning, maintaining, and assessing curricula.

Aspirational peers are programs that succeed in doing something relevant to current practice, particular philosophical perspectives on design, or difficult educational challenges. These schools define best practices and set standards for others. While it is important to be realistic in selecting aspirational peers—for example, accounting for some similarities in resources, types of degree offerings, or student populations—it is also important to identify which institutions set the pace for design education. Faculty look to aspirational peers for a variety of reasons but rarely to copy curriculum. Curriculum design is a context-specific activity. Instead, aspirational peers represent a yardstick for measuring how forward thinking, effective, or efficient a program is in some aspect of curricular, pedagogical, or operational activities. These peers represent concrete examples for addressing new ideas circulating in the field. Studying the work of peers also identifies gaps in perspectives or approaches that may be new opportunities for program development.

It is also crucial to understand the peer competition for students within a geographic region or among types of schools. While graduate students tend to select institutions for access to particular faculty or perspectives on design study, undergraduates choose schools for a wider variety of reasons, including location or preparation for a specific kind of work. Therefore, faculty should understand the diversity of missions among schools in the same market for design study. It makes little sense to pursue the curricular mission of another successful institution in the region. Further, certain areas of the country support some missions better than others. For example, a program that focuses on exhibition design may do better in a large city with a number of museums that offer internship possibilities for students than in a small town.

A Few Words on National Rankings

Different countries use different strategies for ranking institutions and disciplinary programs. College and university rankings began in the early twentieth century and are driven by the transition to knowledge-intensive economies, global pursuit of talent, increasing importance of higher education to the economy and society, and consumerist attitudes toward selecting schools (Hazelkorn, 2015). Ranking by an independent entity addresses the absence of institutionally generated comparative data, particularly in the sciences. Since its inception, nations have experimented with methods for choosing indicators of success, weighting them, and communicating accurate results.

In the United States, the dominant method for ranking schools and programs is by reputation surveys, such as those employed by *US News and World Report* and *DesignIntelligence*. Reputation surveys depend on top-of-the-mind impressions held by respondents, not on any systematic review of curricular outcomes or any verification of institutional descriptions. In ranking MFA programs, for example, *USNWR* asks an administrator from each institution (often a dean) to list the top ten programs nationally in a number of individual art and design disciplines. There is no guarantee that the respondent has any direct experience with programs in their lists or with the schools' students or faculty. Programs that offer graduate study under alternate terminal degree titles, such as a two-year Master of Design degree, are not included among institutional options in this survey, even when they have high reputations for curricular success and meet requirements for the terminal degree. There have been instances in which a school is ranked at the top of a discipline by

USNWR even though the institution offers no degree study in that field; survey respondents merely assumed that the high–reputation school must be good at everything. *USNWR* does not appear to do any follow–up research to confirm survey opinions.

Other countries use different indicators and methods, with an increasing number employing user–centered searches for particular institutional characteristics and no holistic ranking of schools. *The College Scorecard*, developed by the US government under the Obama administration, uses this approach and provides federal data for a number of important indicators as ways of gaining more nuanced understanding of institutions. The ultimate goal of any ranking system should be for students to find the program that best matches their educational aspirations and qualifications.

Therefore, using reputation–driven rankings may not be the best means for faculty selecting aspirational peers. Despite the tendency of college presidents to see improved rankings as important to their institutions, faculty should identify peer programs through meaningful inquiry and real indicators of success.

Faculty frequently argue that while tools may change, design principles remain stable over time. This implies that projection is mostly about addressing new technical skills, rather than looking for challenges to assumptions on which curriculum is based. As a result, programs often maintain the same curricular structure and content, while adding new competencies at the end of under–graduate course sequences. Before long the curriculum is overloaded and beginning courses no longer prepare students for study at the upper levels.

In *The Structure of Scientific Revolutions*, historian Thomas Kuhn described "normal science" as one in which a single paradigm dominates the discipline. He warns that such paradigms "gain their status because they are more successful than others in solving a few problems that practitioners have come to recognize as being acute" (Kuhn, 1970, p. 23). Practice often extends knowledge that "matches the paradigm's predictions by further articulation of the paradigm" (Kuhn, 1970, p. 23). In other words, rather than search for a new paradigm, the practice simply expands the conceptual territory of the existing paradigm to account for novel problems and outcomes. We see some of this expansion in the current interest in design thinking, under a presumption that the same principles used to generate successful artifacts can be used to transform businesses, reform education, and solve social problems. Similarly, some educators and practitioners view interaction design as print design moved to the screen with sound and motion as additional variables, rather than a new, symmetrical relationship between designer and audience. It is likely that these recent practices require an alternative paradigm that has profound implications for curriculum design.

Projection should do more than identify potential content additions to curricula based on the "normal science" of design. It should examine the relevance of all content knowledge and ask questions about the underlying assumptions that form the basis of existing curricular and pedagogical approaches. It should identify anomalies that do not fit current practices and examine emerging "cultures of practice" that represent shifting paradigms in the professions that curricula serve.

PLANNING FOR PROGRAM EFFECTIVENESS

Curriculum planning is the consensus-building process through which faculty articulate the values, content, activities, and evidence they believe will address the needs of students and the strategic environment for design practice. It is a means for ensuring that faculty understand the role courses play in a larger educational effort and for informing administrative perspectives for the allocation of resources, management of enrollment, and assessment of program performance.

Components nested within a curriculum plan are:

- Mission statement
- Goals and objectives
- Learning outcomes, evidence, and measures
- Pedagogies and projects
- Assessment strategies

Mission Statement

A mission statement describes the purpose of a program and its view on the intellectual discipline and practice of design. It is an articulation of intent and steers the recruitment of students and the long-range planning, implementation, and assessment of curricular activities by faculty. At the program level, the mission should be consistent with the overall vision of the institution, but it should also reflect what the faculty think about design in particular.

It is easy to view authorship of a mission statement as an administrative exercise—as satisfying a pesky institutional requirement with something lofty that will be forgotten quickly under more pressing demands.

I ask graduate students in a class on teaching to review the mission statements of well-known design programs, copied from college and university websites. Students don't know the names of the schools, even though some are the very institutions from which they graduated. I then ask them to describe the character of the curriculum they would expect to arise from the mission statements they reviewed. For example, if a school publishes a mission to prepare students for entry to professional practice, we might guess that it offers a professional degree with significant work in the discipline, possibly including internship and capstone opportunities. If the mission statement describes deep concern for the contribution of design to culture and the human condition, students might assume that humanities and social sciences content plays some important role in the curriculum. If the mission statement emphasizes the relationship between design and the natural environment, students might expect issues of sustainability to appear in more than one course description.

Once graduate students articulate their best guess regarding the character of the corresponding curriculum, they receive the names of the institutions and compare their analyses to published course descriptions. More often than not, mission statements are so general as to be uninformative regarding curricular expectations or bear little resemblance to the curricular content as delivered. In some cases, students don't even recognize the mission statement of their alma mater, whose curricula they know intimately.

The point of this exercise is to illustrate that mission statements should communicate to students, parents, employers, accreditors, and the rest of the institution the vision and values that guide educational decision-making by faculty and their program administration. Writing a mission statement is an activity through which faculty negotiate and express collective aspirations and priorities among all of the things design education could be. In this way, mission statements indicate the degree of clarity and insight in the faculty's views on design, as well as the philosophical underpinnings of curriculum and instruction. The purpose of writing a mission statement is not to satisfy an institutional requirement but to reach agreement among faculty regarding curricular principles and intent, often unvoiced in previous discussions.

Well-conceived mission statements have several characteristics in common. First, they reflect purposes, philosophies, and values about student learning in design that are likely to persist over time. While they are antici-patory of changes in the strategic environment and informed through pro-jection activities, they generally address issues that transcend temporary or minor modulations in the culture. Programs should not rewrite their mission statements every year. They should decide what is likely to endure in the face of short-term changes in practice and education.

Second, effective mission statements are distinctive enough to separate the program from others—both in design and in other disciplines—and to clearly reflect a position within the range of possible perspectives on the field and edu-cation. The mission statement should tell a prospective student what it means to study design in the program and reflect how outcomes are different from or similar to other programs that offer the same degree. Many programs, for example, want students to be "professionally prepared" but will differ radically in what they think that means. For some, it is simply qualifying for any entry-level position in the field. For others, it is the ability to evolve with a changing prac-tice over time. And given the diversification of the field, there are many flavors of practice that make it impossible for a single program to serve all equally well.

Mission statements should use language that suggests particular goals and objectives and that infers criteria for evaluating success. Everyone today wants students to "innovate," but what does that really mean for the design and eval-uation of curriculum? In Figure 2.3, a program identifies systems-level prob-lem-solving as integral to innovation. It further describes complex systems as having environmental, technological, economic, cultural, and social dimen-sions and innovative solutions as being sustainable, feasible, viable, desirable, and responsible. In other words, using everyday language and a few sentences, the statement sets an educational agenda and implies standards for how cur-riculum must perform.

Of recent concern in the field is clear differentiation between the missions of undergraduate liberal arts and professional degrees and between under-graduate and graduate study. In some design disciplines, such as architecture and landscape architecture, the type of undergraduate degree determines the path to licensure: students must follow four-year preprofessional degrees with additional study in an accredited professional bachelor of architecture/land-scape architecture or a master of architecture/landscape architecture program to qualify for professional internships and to sit for licensure exams. These fields also regulate the use of the titles "architect" and "landscape architect" through degree qualifications.

FIGURE 2.3 *Nesting of mission, goals, and objectives.*

Mission statement: The design program prepares undergraduate students to shape emerging practices in the design field through innovative, systems-level design solutions that are environmentally sustainable, technologically feasible, economically viable, culturally desirable, and socially responsible.

Goal 1: Improve students' preparation for work in the design of user-centered, technologically networked systems.

Objective A: Students will conduct research to inform the design of networked experiences.

Outcome A1: Students will make appropriate choices among research methods for determining users' cognitive, cultural, and social differences.

Outcome A2: Students will visually document and critically evaluate the range of settings and tasks in which users interact with relevant networked systems.

Objective B: Students will frame design problems in terms of complex, user-centered systems.

Outcome B1: Students will describe system components and analyze the nature of the relationships among them in complete and coherent form.

Outcome B2: Students will identify and justify leverage points for systems intervention in which small changes make big improvements in user satisfaction.

Outcome B3: Students will present a clearly articulated communication brief for an interdisciplinary team that ranks design priorities in terms of user experience.

In other design disciplines—such as communication, industrial, and interior design—the distinctions between *liberal arts* and *professional* degree programs generally reside in the distribution of credits across four years of study that are seen by the field as necessary to achieve professional competencies. Accreditation of BA/BS curricula generally indicates that less than 65 percent of the total coursework is in art and design, with the remainder of the curriculum in liberal arts study. The profession and accreditating committees typically consider liberal arts degrees as preprofessional, meaning that their missions should focus on design within the context of general studies, even when programs advertise a design major within BA/ BS degrees.

BFA programs in art with an *emphasis* or *concentration* in a design discipline show 65 percent or more of the coursework in art and design but too few credits in a specific design discipline and its history for a major that develops the full range of competencies required for professional practice.

Professional degrees with a full *major* in a design discipline—such as the BFA in industrial design or the Bachelor of Graphic Design—require at least 65 percent of the curriculum in art and design study and 25 percent or more study in the design major. In these programs, students are immersed in the design discipline with the possibility of some elective work in other areas. Accrediting agencies and professional associations generally consider these as *first professional degrees*.

While some graduates of liberal arts degrees in design gain employment in design fields, they have lower practice-oriented qualifications than their BFA peers. Faculty frequently argue that this employment is evidence of the program as a professional degree. The reality, however, is that completing as few as fifteen credits in the discipline simply cannot make students professionally competitive with BFA students who undertake eighty or more credits in design. The design fields need some meaningful distinction between these differently qualified student populations. A first job in design may not require citation of design history in day-to-day work, for example, but understanding precedence is one competency that separates a professional from a nonprofessional. And while painting and drawing may inform a designer's work, it doesn't replace the need for other knowledge and skills such as user-based research, manufacturing and production processes, or the design of large-scale technological systems. Therefore, what students do after graduation is not the only determinant of a professional degree.

The missions of liberal arts programs, therefore, should be significantly different from those of professional degree offerings—not "professional lite"— because students typically don't have the opportunity to acquire the full range of knowledge and skills that allows them to evolve a dynamic practice—to be change agents within their fields. Further, programs should communicate these differences in mission to students in recruitment, advising, and program literature. Students should not learn of the professional limitations of their preparation during a job interview. This is not to say that broadly educated

students in liberal arts degree programs in design can't make meaningful contributions to practice, but it is the responsibility of the program to define an
attractive mission that articulates the specific nature of these contributions as
distinct from those of degrees with significantly more professional content.

Equally confusing in many institutions are the differing missions of undergraduate and graduate programs in design. Following the tradition in fine arts
education and the history addressed in chapter 1 of this book, the content of
master's programs in design often focuses on deepening and refining knowledge and skills acquired through undergraduate study. In some programs,
graduate students develop through largely independent work or through
coregistration in courses designed for a dominant population of upper-level
undergraduates. It is also common for architecture and design programs to
admit students with no previous design study or limited undergraduate backgrounds in the discipline, allowing them to "catch up" through master's offerings that prepare them generally for entry-level positions.

Because the Master of Fine Arts—or its equivalent in curricular requirements under a design-oriented title, such as Master of Architecture, Master of
Interior Design, Master of Industrial Design, or Master of Graphic Design—is
considered the *terminal degree* in the United States, it implies that graduates
possess the knowledge to teach design at the college level upon graduation.
When master's programs fail to address missions more focused and ambitious
than entry-level employment for change-of-career students, they handicap
graduates as leaders in practice and as faculty in the research-intensive climate
of today's higher education. This is not to say that change-of-career applicants
should be rejected for graduate study or that *initial master's degrees* (MA/MS
degrees) don't have a role to play in an array of degree offerings. And in many
schools, change-of-career students enroll for three to four years, surpassing
basic skills in the upper levels of their master's study. However, it is the norm
in all other disciplines that advanced degrees are distinctly different in content
and expectations from undergraduate programs and not simply a shorter route
to basic employment skills for students who have met the general education
requirements of an undergraduate degree.

Also exerting pressure on graduate curricula is the level at which design
is now practiced. In many companies today, design is a strategic business operation or an interdisciplinary partner in the company's research and development activities. As such, the expertise required of designers is more than
students can acquire through undergraduate study. Focused master's programs

often build this expertise through intensive study that departs from the traditional fine arts studio model.

Within recent decades, universities have also developed doctoral programs in design to meet accelerating expectations for expertise. The professional doctorate (for example, the Doctor of Architecture) deepens professional competencies and serves an audience of experienced practitioners who reflect on issues facing contemporary practice. By contrast, the PhD in design is currently a research degree in the United States. It addresses the generation of evidence-based knowledge that informs the field through dissertation work and the publication of research findings.

The separation of these two doctoral missions is less clear in Europe. The 1999 Bologna Accord upwardly reclassified institutions and degrees, allowing residents of one European country to qualify for further study and employment in another. Previously, higher education systems in various European countries differed widely in their levels of study, making academic and professional mobility across national boundaries difficult. Out of the accord emerged several doctoral missions for European schools. *Practice-based PhDs* have missions roughly equivalent to professional doctorates in the United States. In some cases, the rigor of these programs is not significantly different from ambitious master's programs in the United States that require reflective documentation of a studio-based project. Other PhD programs in Europe are *evidence-based* and have the mission of producing empirical knowledge under required coursework in a cognate and systematic research methods comparable to those in nondesign fields. These are not studio programs. And still other programs offer a *PhD through publication* requiring no specific coursework or study of research methods and as few as fifteen contact hours with faculty per year. Because these various missions operate under the same degree title—PhD—it is difficult for universities and employers to determine the likely content of a candidate's doctoral experience.

It is important, therefore, for programs to be precise about their missions and to describe them consistently across recruitment activities, advising, and institutional literature.

Goals, Objectives, and Outcomes

Program goals are broad, long-range statements of intent. Collectively, they describe overarching principles and general concepts that guide curriculum development and assessment. Missions persist, but goals must be monitored to ensure their continuing relevance.

In Figure 2.3, the program example identifies systems-level problem-solving as part of its mission. Goal 1 focuses on the curricular implications of systems-oriented work in the design of networked technology, an "emerging practice." In other words, there is a direct connection between the goal and the mission.

Objectives are more specific than goals. They define the student competencies necessary for goal achievement, describing what faculty expect students to know, value, and be able to do. In some cases, the learning expressed in objectives is a matter of achieving or not achieving threshold proficiency. A communication design student either does or doesn't know how to code in HTML. An interior design student does or does not know the differences among plans, elevations, and sections. In other instances, faculty expect to see a range of competencies among students or progressive improvement by individual students over time with respect to the objective. In Figure 2.3, faculty declare that conducting user-centered research and framing design problems are essential competencies for work in the design of networked systems. Research skills develop over time, and different students will show lesser and greater skills in framing problems. In other words, measuring student performance in these cases will require more detailed explanations of the competencies than can be found in the objective alone.

Learning outcomes are even more precise than objectives and describe: 1) the acquisition of knowledge, skills, and dispositions expected of students; 2) the ways in which students will demonstrate these competencies; and 3) criteria for evaluating student success. Faculty write learning outcomes at the level of curriculum, courses, and projects (Figure 2.4).

Well-written learning outcomes exhibit several important characteristics in structure and content:

- *Outcomes define student learning*: Learning outcomes describe what students should know and be able to do as a result of their education. Outcomes are not what faculty do in their delivery of content or an inventory of the subject matter to be taught. Neither are they descriptions of procedures that students follow in executing learning tasks (Figure 2.4).

FIGURE 2.4 *Writing learning outcomes.*

VERSION 1: Students will know the five historic classifications of typeface design.

- No description of observable behavior. *Knowing* can't be observed, however, *identifying* and *describing* can.
- No criteria for judging levels of student performance.
- Focuses on content, not on the enduring design competency that the content represents.

VERSION 2: Students will draft letterforms from the five major classifications of typeface design, annotate drawings with descriptions of defining characteristics, and use each typeface in the design of a magazine spread.

- Describes procedures not competencies. Doesn't indicate the intent of these activities.
- No criteria for judging levels of student performance that tell students what is expected and faculty what standards should be used in evaluating student work.
- Conflates too many things in the same outcome.

VERSION 3: Students will critically analyze how historic precedence and the expressive characteristics of a typeface design make it an appropriate choice in particular applications.

- Describes an observable/measurable behavior (*analyze*).
- Implies why the the knowledge is important and how it might be demonstrated in practice.
- Suggests criteria for evaluation (*criticality* and judgments of *appropriateness*) that can define different levels of student performance.
- Leaves open a number of ways to structure student activities to achieve the objective.

Faculty have a tendency to author course objectives and learning outcomes in instructional terms, implying that if they execute the plan the program will succeed in its mission. If the only things outcomes address are faculty tasks or an inventory of content to be taught, on what evidence does the program report success? The only possible answer to "How are we doing as a curriculum in executing the mission?" is "We taught important subject matter and provided good instruction," not that students achieved some level of competency.

Neither are outcomes procedural. They focus on learning, not on a sequence of steps students complete to reach proficiency. Procedural descriptions also present problems in assessing student achievement. The only answer to "Did students master the desired competencies?" is "They did (or didn't) execute the tasks faculty assigned."

Outcomes tell students what faculty expect in the content and qualities of their performance. They should be evident and consistent across course syllabi, project briefs, and grading rubrics. Two of the most frequent complaints by students in their evaluations of instruction are that the purpose of an assignment was never apparent or that expectations of their performance shifted across the duration of the project.

- *Outcomes describe observable behaviors*: Learning outcomes use action verbs (Figure 2.5). Faculty can't observe "understanding" or "appreciation," but they can make judgments about students' ability to explain or hold a perspective on a design issue. They can evaluate the accuracy, completeness, and coherence of an explanation. They can determine whether students developed a perspective through critical consideration of alternatives or blindly adopted an easily accessible theory. In other words, there are observable behaviors that are evidence of understanding and appreciation, as well as levels of acceptable performance associated with each behavior.

- *Outcomes imply standards for assessment*: Well-written learning outcomes suggest rubrics for assessing student achievement. Rubrics define a graded structure of expectations faculty use in evaluating student work. Learning outcomes should describe criteria that distinguish one student's performance from another's.

It is a common practice to describe levels of learning in a topical area as *Beginning, Intermediate, and Advanced* or *Design I, II, and III*. Rather than define discrete competencies for each course, outcomes are written as, "Students will continue development of skills acquired in Design I" or "Students will apply skills X, Y, and Z to more advanced problems."

This approach to curriculum design implies scaffolded levels of accomplishment but often leaves individual faculty to determine the distinctions that separate beginning from advanced work. Defining courses primarily through their position in a sequence can easily

Adapt	Diagram	Organize
Analyze	Differentiate	Persuade
Apply	Discover	Plan
Appraise	Discuss	Practice
Arrange	Distinguish	Predict
Articulate	Employ	Prepare
Assemble	Evaluate	Present
Assess	Examine	Prioritize
Calculate	Experiment	Produce
Categorize	Explain	Propose
Choose	Express	Question
Classify	Extend	Rank
Collaborate	Facilitate	Recognize
Collect	Generalize	Record
Combine	Generate	Refine
Compare	Give examples of	Relate
Compose	Identify	Report
Conclude	Illustrate	Represent
Connect	Interpret	Research
Construct	Intervene	Review
Contrast	Interview	Sketch
Create	Invent	Solve
Critique	Judge	Specify
Decide on/to	Justify	Speculate
Defend	List	State
Define	Manage	Structure
Demonstrate	Manipulate	Summarize
Depict	Map	Test
Describe	Modify	Trace
Design	Name	Transform
Devise	Observe	Visualize

FIGURE 2.5 *Faculty cannot observe "understanding" or "appreciation," but they can discern actions that are evidence of these aspects of learning. When writing learning outcomes with assessment in mind, faculty use action verbs that describe observable, measurable behaviors.*

misdirect faculty attention to subject matter and tasks, rather competencies—"Design II is where we do project X or activity Y"—without truly agreeing on a developmental progression of specific aptitudes across multiple courses. It is not unusual, for example, for different faculty to replicate essentially the same design challenge—with minor changes in user or medium—across several semesters. In other words, when course descriptions fail to include specific learning outcomes that describe discrete competencies, the logic of the curriculum design is unclear to both faculty and students.

- *Outcomes are realistic in number.* Outcomes can be written for curricula, courses, and projects. Each requires a different degree of specificity. Curricular outcomes are typically framed as general exit competencies shown by students as they graduate or reach designated milestones in the course of study. Course outcomes reflect the particular contribution a course makes to the development of curricular competencies. Project outcomes describe the expectations of discrete assignments. It is important to maintain this hierarchy, or outcomes proliferate beyond what is reasonable for the duration of study at each level.

Pedagogies and Projects

Unlike goals, objectives, and outcomes, pedagogies and projects are variable and often left to the discretion of individual faculty. Chapter 3 of this book deals with these aspects of teaching and learning in greater detail. In terms of planning, however, there should be coordination among faculty regarding instructional strategies. For example, faculty may agree that early studies are comprised of short projects and exercises rather than comprehensive solutions to larger problems. Or they may recommend front-loading technological instruction in the first weeks of the semester rather than just-in-time learning across the course.

Difficulty in curriculum planning often arises from faculty who are tied to particular pedagogies and projects, irrespective of newly negotiated learning objectives and outcomes. These faculty engage in planning work by looking for where to locate favorite assignments and assuming continuation of familiar instructional approaches, despite the collective intent to send the program in new directions. Programs with strong planning cultures share syllabi and assess outcomes regularly, with everyone accountable to a common vision.

Evidence and Measures

Later sections of this book discuss assessment strategies in detail, but planning efforts should anticipate the kind of evidence faculty expect to collect in determining the effectiveness of the curriculum and instruction; the places and timing of that evidence collection; and descriptions of acceptable levels of student performance.

For example, if a curricular objective states that "students will frame problems and solutions in terms of user experience," then concept maps that describe the relationships among various users, activities, and settings might be appropriate evidence of such awareness in sophomores. Faculty need not assess all curricular objectives/outcomes in all courses all the time. Checking to see if seniors use experience mapping in independent projects—and if so, how integral the map is to their analyses of problems—provides a second touch point for evaluating the objective. And faculty may look at this objective across several cohorts and then move on to other competencies in subsequent years. The key is to be systematic in collecting evidence of student performance, which requires agreement among faculty.

Further, faculty must decide what level of student performance is acceptable in achieving curricular objectives and outcomes. For example, do all students in the beginning course need to construct a concept map that shows both *breadth* and *depth* in user-centered issues as an essential competency for advancement? Or is this a competency that develops over time with some students showing mastery later in their studies? If the latter, then how well must sophomores perform to ensure that seniors exhibit acceptable exit skills? While it may be appropriate for the majority of students to be proficient in a skill as sophomores, with a few students developing competency, the program may expect mastery of the skill as a graduation threshold for all seniors. In planning the type and timing of evidence collection, faculty ensure that assessment takes place and that findings are based on comparable measures of performance and outcomes valued by all faculty.

RESPONDING TO THE DEMAND FOR CURRICULAR FLEXIBILITY

Rapidly evolving design practices present particular challenges for maintaining the relevancy of undergraduate design curricula. Technologies constantly reconfigure workflow. Changing patterns in social and cultural behavior encourage new areas of design practice. Fluctuations in business demand new insights that expand the accountability for design. Entry-level expectations of employers often shift before a student cohort completes a four-year degree. For institutions with lengthy curricular approval processes, keeping up with practice can be daunting, and it is not surprising that faculty tend to solve this problem through incremental course additions at the upper levels of undergraduate curricula or completely disregard the course of study as planned and

Rapidly changing professions / slow curricular approval processes become a problem when faculty define courses solely by temporarily relevant content, theories, and skills, rather than concepts and methods that are enduring.

Decreasing budgets / expanding design enrollments often produce less diversity in course offerings in favor of more sections and fewer opportunities to experiment with new content.

Curriculum-by-accrual strategies for adding new content often lead to a cafeteria of courses defined by segments of practice with no overarching perspective that establishes relationships among offerings or guides choices of what to retain and what to let go.

Marketing incentives for increasing undergraduate degree specialization commit programs to currently popular curricula with no assurance that matching professional practices will persist.

Cult-of-personality teaching results in no curricular logic or unifying perspective that guides responses to changing conditions; faculty battle over whether change is necessary and how to bring it about.

Faculty specialization and ownership of courses make it difficult to shift the emphasis of a curriculum when new expertise is missing or existing courses are outdated roadblocks to change.

Overly rigid adherence to traditional scheduling and staffing turns everything into 16 weeks of instruction with fewer than 20 students under a single faculty member, making new offerings costly in terms of resources and space in the curriculum.

Misperceptions of curricular mandates lead faculty to believe each competency requires a discrete course; faculty quickly run of out room in the curriculum.

FIGURE 2.6 *If not addressed, obstacles to flexibility contribute to declining program relevance and faculty frustration in limited opportunities in innovation. Programs really want curricula that are agile, anticipatory of changes in the field, open to individual faculty contributions, and manageable in scope and scale.*

published. It is common, for example, for faculty to tell external curriculum reviewers to ignore the course catalog because it no longer matches what they do in the classroom.

There are a number of obstacles to designing adaptive curricula that respond effectively to frequent changes in the strategic environment for design (Figure 2.6). Despite general agreement among faculty that the conditions for practice have changed, these obstacles often result in declining curricular effectiveness, decreasing clarity regarding program mission, faculty frustration over few opportunities to innovate, and/or too much to teach in too little

Advertising design	Logo/visual identity design
Book design	Magazine design/print, online
Branding	Mobile/small screen design
Broadcast design	Motion graphics/main titles
Communication strategy	Newspaper design
Corporate collateral	Package design
Direct mail/marketing design	Poster design
Exhibition design	Service design
Experience design	Signage design/wayfinding
Game design	Social design/public service
Icon/symbol design	Software and platform design
Illustration	Textbook/educational media
Information design/mapping	Typeface design
Interaction design	Web design
Interface design	

FIGURE 2.7 *Constructing curricula from segments of professional practice or products that designers make discourages faculty from agreeing on a progression of overall student competencies in the four-year course of study. Further, a finite number of credits for graduation requires faculty to include some practices and ignore others. The result is a "cafeteria" of curricular offerings that is rarely complete, predictive of future practice, or deliberately ordered in its development of students' skills and knowledge.*

time. Prolonged failure to address these factors often results in program reality lagging several years behind reputation.

Curricula can be specific about learning outcomes that describe competencies and content likely to endure without locking programs into rigid structures that require constant updating through institutional procedures. Defining curricula by segments of professional practice (Figure 2.7), or the objects students make, places programs at risk of running out of instructional space or committing to professional practices that have short life spans. Further, there is rarely a logical sequence implied by segments of practice. Designing a magazine is not inherently preparatory for designing a website. Designing a vacuum cleaner is not preliminary to designing medical equipment. Designing a retail interior is not a first step to designing a restaurant or a library. This is not to say that topical offerings have no value as means for students to specialize or as elective study, but it is difficult to scaffold a progression of skill development—or to communicate the scaffolding to others—when segments of practice and products define the entire curriculum.

On the other hand, there will always be users or audiences whose experiences of design are cognitive, emotional, and physical. Although the activities that comprise how people work and live will change, they will always reflect motives for engaging with information, objects, and environments. Design always resides within a context defined by physical, social, cultural, technological, and economic factors. Although the specific nature of these conditions may change, the importance of context in solving design problems is a certainty. And while technologies will evolve, all have intrinsic affordances and require that designers make critical judgments about their appropriateness in application. By focusing on these enduring issues and related skills, faculty can build curricula around very particular learning outcomes while still responding to changes in professional practice.

IMPLEMENTING CURRICULAR CHANGE

While each institution has its own procedures for approving curricula, there are several general concerns regarding effective implementation that apply to any program. They include:

- Guaranteed curricular continuity for all students
- Impact forecasting beyond the program
- General and targeted communication about planning and implementation
- Solicitation of feedback and strategies for redirection in response to problems

Because curriculum is a contractual agreement between the student and the institution, all students must have the opportunity to complete the course of study under which they were admitted. This means that programs must decide where, when, and how to introduce new curricular structures and content with the least disruption for students. Such decisions influence student recruitment, admissions criteria, advising, recordkeeping, and any literature that explains degree requirements.

Many institutions have experimental course numbers under which faculty can offer instruction not yet incorporated into curricular requirements. Programs often accept these courses as electives, allowing faculty to test new content, structures, and instructional methods with particular groups of students without displacing the existing curriculum. In some programs, students in these courses are graded pass/fail to protect them from the perils of new instruction.

Other institutions develop "tracks" or certificate offerings that cluster a series of new courses as focused study within a major with the goal of eventually replacing or expanding core offerings. This approach to introducing new content and skills was popular as digital technology changed many design practices. Coding and time-based work, for example, appeared as elective skill sets as traditional art and design disciplines shifted to interactive media and computer-assisted design. The risk in this approach, however, is that tracks often become independent majors, leaving the parent curriculum without the benefit of new knowledge and the new program lacking in foundational concepts in deference to immediately marketable skills. It is attractive for faculty steeped in traditional practices and media to hire new colleagues to provide instruction in emerging issues. But when these new faculty seek some curricular autonomy, curricula can artificially segregate content that is fully integrated under current professional practice.

In other cases, programs phase in the introduction of a new curriculum across time, beginning with an entering student cohort while maintaining the old curriculum until returning students graduate. Students are often given the option to complete their degrees under either curriculum, although the institution is obligated to students who want to finish the course of study under which they entered. This approach means that programs must differentiate advising and recordkeeping practices and decide how to accommodate students who cannot complete coursework under typical patterns of registration.

It is also helpful to forecast the impact of curriculum changes on enrollment. In many cases, curriculum revisions open the program to new audiences. In other instances, they shift patterns of registration away from more traditional courses or other majors. For example, the implementation of an interaction design curriculum may draw students away from a more traditional, print-based graphic design curriculum. Curricular changes also affect the type of students who apply to the program. An interaction design curriculum may attract technologically oriented students who would never apply to a traditional arts-based program. How the program recruits and evaluates the qualifications of new student populations is an important part of implementation.

The introduction of curricular change can be unsettling to students. For students in the new curriculum, the future is unknown. Students in the older curriculum frequently question the continuing relevance or value of the original degree program. Therefore, how the program introduces a new plan is crucial to its success. Meetings with students to explain the curriculum, reasons for change, and future activities in its implementation are essential. Throughout the implementation process, it is helpful to engage students in evaluation. "How are we doing" discussions allow faculty to make mid-course changes that respond to student feedback.

ASSESSING CURRICULAR CHANGE

In terms of the projection–planning–delivery–assessment cycle, it is important to sustain an ongoing evaluative process that informs projection and planning. It is also crucial that programs nest an assessment strategy within institutional expectations and carry it out consistently from year to year. In other words, an approach to assessment is designed, not a matter of faculty's anecdotal accounts of "pretty good classes in design." Assessment plans often include the following:

- Rubrics that describe graded levels of acceptable student performance
- Methods and sources for collecting evidence on outcomes
- Timing of evidence collection
- Use of results

If well written, learning outcomes identify the observable performances expected of successful students. *Rubrics* describe a graded continuum of individual student performance from poor to excellent. Faculty and students should understand both the learning outcomes and the corresponding rubrics for evaluation. There should be no difference in reporting to students, faculty, and the institution regarding how well students do in meeting curricular and course expectations. Some programs use the learning outcomes and rubrics for individual courses as a format for structuring critiques and reporting grades to students. Where things go wrong is when programs develop an entirely new set of curricular expectations for an institutional assessment exercise from the criteria used in the program throughout the year.

It is common for universities to have an office of assessment that sets the format for evaluation of curricula. Institutional formats and metrics tend to favor statistical data (enrollment, faculty-to-student ratios, credit-hour production, satisfaction surveys, grade distributions, retention and graduate rates, and so forth). Many of today's universities also use software that calls for periodic submissions of data common to all academic units. In general, these reporting formats reduce outcomes to descriptions so brief as to be ineffective in driving curricular projection and planning in the discipline. And in the interest of institutional comparisons across programs, many criteria lack sensitivity to the issues faculty deem most important to teaching and learning in their fields.

While it is unlikely that design programs can opt out of participation in these standardized evaluations, it is important to conduct other types of assessment that the program values and to report results to administration through various channels, such as annual reports and summaries of student achievements. In many cases, accredited programs use the national accreditation standards for design programs as their curricular outcomes to avoid duplicate assessment efforts and to demonstrate consistency with national benchmarks. In this way, accreditation self-studies and interim reports to the institution are consistent in what they measure.

Typically, design faculty engage in much more assessment than faculty in nonvisual programs. Every critique, for example, requires expert judgment about how well students do in achieving stated outcomes. Many programs have mid-program reviews of students for advancement to upper-level coursework. And the review of portfolios is a long-standing practice in design, while the rest of the academy has just discovered their value in assessing student progress and programs over time. Design programs, however, are notoriously remiss in articulating and documenting all the evaluation activities they routinely undertake. Chapter 6 of this book describes assessment strategies in greater detail. It is crucial, however, that projection and planning are informed by assessment results in a cycle of continuous improvement.

SUMMARY

Designing and monitoring curriculum effectiveness require projection, planning, implementation, and assessment. Good curriculum plans include a mission statement, goals and objectives, student learning outcomes, evidence and measures, and assessment strategies. Success depends on faculty reaching consensus about content and pedagogical strategy, disciplined and systematic attention to curricular details, and documentation that attributes outcomes to specific practices. In light of the changing conditions of contemporary practice described in chapter 1, it is time for faculty to question the continuing relevance of traditional approaches to curriculum and instruction, to innovate as designers of learning experiences.

CHAPTER 3:
PEDAGOGIES AND PROJECTS

Passing the studios every evening, our chancellor asked how design faculty convince students to work in university classrooms long after the school day ends. For many students, the design studio represents the first formal education configured to match the way they prefer to learn. It is a place that teaches enterprise—eagerness to undertake new ventures—not school subjects.

THE SIGNATURE PEDAGOGY OF DESIGN

Pedagogy is the method or practice of teaching. It is both art and science. As president of the Carnegie Foundation, Lee Shulman described *signature pedagogies* as characteristic forms of instruction used to develop future practitioners or scholars within a field. He suggested that these pedagogies transform content knowledge and are particularly distinct in professional education because they are accountable for supporting "accomplished and responsible practice in the service of others" (Shulman, 2005, p. 53).

Shulman studied the contradictions between the various roles played by professionals and the ways in which their education prepared them for practice. He used engineering as an example. In teaching fluid dynamics, the professor lectured from the podium, then spent the remainder of the class writing on the board while students copied formulas for discussion in self-organized study groups after class. Shulman described this teaching strategy as lacking a strong relationship between knowing and doing in engineering (Shulman, 2005). On the other hand, in the engineering design studio, groups of students worked in activity areas with no apparent orientation to an authority figure. They engaged with physical models, collaborated on projects, built things, and critiqued peers' work. The professor moved around the room but only as encouragement and a secondary source of information. This was the signature pedagogy of engineering. Shulman argued that signature pedagogies are important because they represent a dominant approach to teaching and shape how knowledge is "analyzed, criticized, accepted, or discarded" by the field (Shulman, 2005, p. 54).

Shulman described three dimensions of any pedagogy. The *surface structure* defines the operational aspects of teaching—the typical kinds of faculty demonstrations, questioning and answering, and interactions with students. The *deep structure* represents theory, how to think like a professional, and how to pass on knowledge. The *implicit structure* carries information about professional attitudes and values (Shulman, 2005, p. 55).

As in engineering, the studio embodies the signature pedagogy of design. Its *surface structure* is defined by projects, communicated through faculty-authored briefs and introductory presentations that describe the scope of work as well as constraints and opportunities in a design challenge. Projects frequently resemble professional assignments and require the types of interactions professionals have with clients, users, and colleagues. Faculty also interact with students in technical demonstrations, desk critiques, and discussions of relevant concepts. As chapter 1 of this book illustrated, there is a long educational lineage that established this surface structure, and, more recently, other college disciplines have copied it to overcome the limitations of large lecture classes.

The *deep structure* of design pedagogy is reflected both in the way projects immerse students in the overarching questions of the discipline and the process-oriented work of practice. Faculty typically structure beginning projects to illustrate principles of design. Unlike work in professional offices, these assignments often distort the importance of a concept or skill to demonstrate its effect on the overall outcomes of design. Students are likely to encounter the same content in later projects but under an alternate ranking of priorities. It is through the repetition and shuffling of relationships among variables in constantly changing problem contexts that students build design knowledge. This approach is in contrast to other disciplinary pedagogies under which students master theories and skills before using them in the practical work of the field. A chemistry student, for example, acquires basic understanding of mathematics and the molecular structure of elements before ever doing the work of a chemist. In design, mastery emerges from doing the work of the field, from solving problems at the very first level of the curriculum.

Design faculty rarely deliver discrete lessons on the design process. Instead, process is embedded in the deep structure of the pedagogy through projects that demand particular kinds of thinking and action. Observations of people and settings, for example, are ways in which designers learn about the experiences of others. Diagramming and sketching are processes through which they refine hazy impressions in the mind and communicate ideas to others. Prototyping is propositional. It confirms the designers' predictions of use and the effects of external forces. Collectively, these experiences build students' understanding of process. Almost any design student can describe the design process, but few remember a specific course or lecture designed to teach it.

Today's interest in design thinking by management and education has produced a number of efforts to describe the design process as a series of discrete steps that can be applied to any problem. The result is often preoccupation with executing steps in a particular order, rather than engaging with important aspects of the challenge and its context through activities and thinking that are especially appropriate to the task. Observation and research, for example, can be found throughout a design process; it is sometimes exploratory, sometimes generative, and sometimes evaluative (Dubberly and Evenson, 2010). Visualization and modeling support consensus-building across many aspects of problem-solving, not just the "making" phase in a linear progression aimed at producing a physical artifact. Design process, therefore, is a multifaceted concept that often unfolds in ways that reflect the particular demands of a problem and its context.

The *implicit structure* of design pedagogy is evident in how faculty frame investigations (what they include or eliminate from the brief), the content of examples they use to support problem definitions, and comments made to students as they work. Design is never bias-free, and faculty impart values and perspectives throughout their interactions with students in the classroom. More than other aspects of instruction, however, the design critique explicitly reinforces the values and priorities of faculty and the field. Lave and Wenger, in their studies of apprenticeship, said, "the purpose is not to learn from talk ... but to learn to talk" as a participant in the work of the domain (Lave and Wenger, 1991, p. 109). Herbert Gans, in his book *Popular Culture and High Culture*, defines *taste cultures* as expressing the values and standards of aesthetics. They result from choice and rarely constitute a total way of life (Gans, 1974).

In many ways, the implicit structure of design pedagogy works to acculturate students in the taste culture of design (Anthony, 1991). Students learn the values of the profession—and by extension, a disciplinary worldview on design and its consequences—through the signature pedagogy of critiques. Faculty can lecture on a range of theories and concepts, but if comments in critiques are inconsistent with lectures, students gravitate to the values expressed in the public evaluation of their work.

Shulman warned that while signature pedagogies are good for developing complex patterns of disciplinary behavior, they are also "dangerous sources of rigidity" that can encourage repetitive responses and distort learning in some respects (Shulman, 2005, p. 56). He cautioned educators that pedagogies often persist "even when they begin to lose their utility, precisely because they are habits with few countervailing forces" (Shulman, 2005, p. 56). Because college-level design faculty rarely receive direct instruction in teaching, they tend to model teaching on their own education, thus reinforcing established pedagogical traditions.

Although the signature pedagogies of design education receive increasing attention from other fields as effective models for teaching and learning, they can be at odds with emerging paradigms in professional design practice. The prevailing model in most communication design programs, for example, is one that supports an art-based, artifact-oriented view of design, despite increasing percentages of professional work in large-scale problems that involve many interdependent variables and systems. Very few communication design programs, for example, structure instruction around issues of behavior, user experience, and complex technological and social systems. Instead, they begin studies with print-based, artifact-centered assignments in the arrangement of form and content and define coursework by what students make, rather than by the nature of the problem. By the third and fourth years of study, the implicit structure of the curriculum has already steeped students in the values of a static, artifact-centered world with asymmetrical relationships between designers and their audiences or users.

It is also common for faculty to strip student investigations of conflicting performance criteria that are seen as compromising "good form." While limiting variables may be appropriate in beginning assignments where students learn the influence of individual factors in shaping design outcomes, it misleads them about the true nature of context as requiring the resolution of competing priorities. Undergraduate design students are *recipients* rather than *framers* of investigations for most of their four years of design study, and if the inherent conflict among constraints is not present in their assignments, they must learn to manage such complexity as professionals when the stakes are much higher.

While some undergraduate programs require independent "thesis" or "capstone" projects—through which students demonstrate the implicit values of practice—curricula typically limit the scope of problems, types of research, and diversity of methods and tools in coursework leading to self-defined work. As a result, in courses that emphasize independent projects, students frequently begin work by identifying an artifact they want to make or struggle for many weeks in defining problem territory—often social or technological—for which they have little knowledge and few skills for addressing systems-level concerns (Davis, 2016).

PEDAGOGICAL STYLES

Most faculty exhibit particular approaches to the signature pedagogy that characterize their work in classrooms. In many cases, pedagogical style is not a conscious choice, and faculty simply do what is comfortable without evaluating the ramifications of how they teach.

Art Direction Approach

An *art-direction approach* leads by faculty example and casts the teacher as an expert in the classroom. This approach is most often used in studios where there is high value assigned to the aesthetic qualities of artifacts. Faculty who direct inexperienced designers in their professional offices are frequently most comfortable with this teaching style as a means for maintaining quality control.

In individual and group critiques, the art-directing faculty member makes explicit suggestions regarding how to improve work—for example, "Create a stronger hierarchy among elements by making headlines bolder and larger" or "Reorient the public spaces along the central spine of the building." In other cases, faculty direct students toward particular solutions through patterns in the praise they give for certain kinds of work. Art direction presumes that managing students' successful solutions to problems models appropriate behavior for future application in practice. Typically, faculty comments include a rationale for suggestions, but the role of the student is still that of an apprentice seeking the master's skill or knowledge within the context of a specific project.

Art direction is an easy way to teach, and it usually yields strong formal results. Faculty who art direct students frequently have the best-looking student work at the end of a semester. The limitation of this approach, however, is that students may not recognize similar concepts in new challenges or contexts. Much like drivers who depend entirely on GPS for navigating roadways, art-directed students may not be able to apply insight from class projects to novel situations because the reasoning required to develop understanding was never activated. It is fairly common, therefore, to find that a consistently art-directed student has work that varies widely in quality under different faculty and from school to the workplace.

A second problem of art direction is that all student work in a class begins to exhibit common visual characteristics, because it doesn't arise from individual student interpretations of the problem or original questions that drive investigations. Not all stylistic consistency is the result of art direction—it may come from peer-to-peer learning or dominant forms in contemporary media—but under an art direction pedagogy, such responses aren't ameliorated by intervening opinions from another source.

Finally, the comments made under an art-direction model for teaching and learning usually spring from a particular design ideology that is rarely revealed to the student or discussed in class. Therefore, the student operates under some vague assumption of "universal truth" and only later learns that his/her design dispositions reside within a spectrum of possible theories or perspectives.

The Socratic Method

The Socratic Method poses questions and encourages students to construct answers. For example, a dialogue intended to develop a student's process for solving problems may go something like this:

Student: I'm having trouble coming up with a solution to this project.

Teacher: What do you think the project is about?

Student: Well, the project brief says we are supposed to be looking at "the relationship between the construction of a message and people's readiness to change a belief or opinion."

Teacher: And what does that suggest to you?

Student: That audiences might be different in what they know about an issue and how willing they are to change?

Teacher: And what do you think might contribute to their openness to change?

Student: Well, some may have had personal experiences with the issue.

Teacher: And what does that mean for how you might go about solving the problem? How would you determine what those experiences are and whether they are meaningful in this particular context?

Student: I guess I'd have to go out and talk to people.

Teacher: What kinds of questions would you ask them?

In extreme examples, every student question is answered by another question. This can be frustrating to beginning students who seek some critical framework from which to make judgments and generate their own questions. Many believe the teacher is simply withholding a known "answer." And while a questioning approach is often useful in kicking off the conceptual end of a project, it may be less appropriate for technical tasks such as learning software or improving craft. Further, the pacing of work across a project usually varies. With beginning students, an endless sequence of questions may not be appropriate at all stages of an activity. Faculty may need to direct action at certain times to maintain the momentum of students' progress.

For more advanced students, especially at the graduate level, the Socratic Method is often used to develop students' personal perspectives on issues or in refining their process. Advanced students are better able to think metacognitively, to reflect on thinking while also addressing the problem parameters.

A risk in the Socratic Method is that students may view all questions and answers as equally valid or appropriate. To be effective, questions need to build critically; they need to model a logic of thought that unfolds as the project progresses and to direct attention to criteria for making judgments. What is being taught under the Socratic Method is an inquiry process that is transferable to any situation. Wiggins and McTighe (2013) discuss the importance of students formulating *essential questions*, of interrogating content. They suggest looking at the work of experts and asking what questions they asked when coming up with answers. For example, in using design history to support studio projects, it may be better for students to ask "How does postmodern work reflect changes in the surrounding culture?" than "What are the stylistic characteristics of postmodern work?" Students must be taught to develop essential questions and to be critical about questions as well as answers. Faculty can model this behavior through their pedagogy.

Coaching Pedagogy

A *coaching pedagogy* falls somewhere in between the faculty as authority figures and as reflective prompts. Under this practice, the faculty member draws student attention to areas of potential investigation that may have been overlooked or misunderstood and suggests general strategies for further development. For example:

Teacher: I see you're struggling with the issue of scale. Let's think about what scale means in this situation. How is it matched to what you hope to accomplish?"

Student: Well, I think the design should reference human scale but also have a sense of importance.

Teacher: So "importance" is reflected in larger-than-life proportions, and users construct that meaning by comparing the size of the space to the size of the human body, by physically experiencing BIG.

Student: Yes.

Teacher: If we were to place two sets of dimensions on a continuum of proportional possibilities for the space, with average human dimensions at one end and this very large space at the other end, what would the intermediate positions on that continuum look like, and just how much contrast would it take for the user to perceive it as meaningful? Could you generate quick sketches that show that spectrum of possibility? And maybe it would be a good idea to mark out these dimensions in an actual environment and experience this scale contrast firsthand.

In what ways can we reference the "importance" of space besides through its scale? Can you brainstorm a list of the possibilities or collect some examples of how other architects have handled that problem of communicating a sense of "importance"?

In this example, the student is neither art directed in a solution to the problem nor left with ambiguity about what the next step might be in reaching conclusions. The faculty member suggests several action-oriented strategies that can be accomplished within a reasonable time frame. Comments offer possible approaches to time management through processes that are quick but exploratory. They also direct attention to a cognitively manageable inventory of issues but leave their resolution to the student. The teacher can step back, let these activities unfold, and then reenter a dialogue about results. It is likely that new insights will emerge, deepening the student's perspective and informing the next teachable moment.

Another aspect in this coaching example is the role the teacher plays in articulating what the student hints is her perception of the design task. The teacher verbally connects for the student the issues of scale and meaning (importance). This idea is embedded in the student's response, but by reasserting it, the teacher validates its worth as a line of inquiry and illustrates how it could drive action. The three suggestions of "next steps" are explicit extensions of the student's perceived interpretation of the problem.

THE TEACHABLE MOMENT

The teachable moment is that time when the student is most prepared to hear what faculty or peers have to say. It may occur when the student has struggled for a while and is not making progress. Although it is tempting to jump in at the first sign of difficulty, a little frustration can be motivating. On the other hand, the teachable moment may be when success in one phase builds confidence that a more difficult task is achievable. Experienced teachers sense when these moments occur and know how to deliver just the right information, demonstration, question, or critique at precisely the right time.

One common characteristic of beginning faculty is an inability to predict the capacity of students to process certain amounts and kinds of information in time. New teachers tend to impart everything they know at once—to direct students to visual examples of solutions before they grasp the scope of the problem or to rush the design process to a polished conclusion when the student is still determining what it means to have a process. Beginning teachers also rely heavily on individual desk critiques, because they have experience in talking one on one about visual work.

The desk critique strategy of classroom management, however, presumes that all students are prepared for a teachable moment at any time in their design process. In some instances, it is better to sequence discussions with students based on their self-declared readiness to talk. In other cases, common misconceptions or patterns of behavior emerge through a series of small critiques with a number of students. In these instances, it makes sense to stop individual conferences and discuss the shared concerns with the group as a whole. It is also possible to suspend work on an assignment and insert an activity that temporarily changes the pace of the class or addresses misunderstanding of something integral to the original project. In other words, the experienced teacher makes decisions regarding the pacing of instruction based on observations of when students need less or more time for reflection on particular issues.

It is equally important to know when students are not prepared to learn. Critiques, for example, are stressful for most students. Some deal with stress by shutting down. Others become defensive. This is particularly characteristic of beginning students who have not learned to separate discussions of their work from perceptions of self-worth. Psychologists describe a phenomenon called *catastrophizing*, predicting a negative outcome and jumping to the conclusion that if it happens, results will be catastrophic. Design students often hear only the negative comments from faculty and peers. Stress, therefore, compromises students' ability to learn from critiques. Assigning a classmate to take notes for the student being critiqued allows the designer to review negative and positive comments under less emotional conditions and provides a checklist of areas that need future work. It is also helpful to collect final projects at the end of one class and critique them at the beginning of the next. This ensures that students have slept and gained some distance before discussing their work.

There is a history of bad pedagogical behavior by faculty that many of today's designers recall as a badge of honor for surviving: faculty tantrums in the classroom, defacing student work, demeaning comments in critiques. Books have been written on the topic and its consequences for students. There is no excuse for a pedagogy of intimidation, and hopefully most of the field has moved beyond this practice, which has roots in the power relationships of the master-apprentice system. In other cases, when instruction appears to have failed, some faculty simply ignore shortfalls in student performance and deal with them in grades when it is too late for students to address concerns. The signature pedagogy of design is unique in most universities and in students' learning histories. It is collaborative and built on mutual trust. When it is clear that students are not responding to instruction, it is best to have calm and open discussions of why and to reach agreement on how to proceed.

There is much discussion in design education about students' missed deadlines. Few topics have spurred more interaction among communication design faculty on the AIGA education listserv than a 2007 discussion of how to penalize students for late work. I lurked on the site for a few days—astounded by the personal affront faculty felt from incomplete work—before weighing in on the culture we perpetuate through personal stories of all-nighters, adrenaline rushes of last-minute solutions, and consistently unreasonable expectations of clients for quick turnaround in professional assignments. Among the most important things to teach students is the nature of a reflective practice, of finding the intellectual challenge in assignments that sustains designers when work seems repetitive, ordinary, or impossible. This often means slowing down the pace of work, engaging in ideas about design rather than simply executing the next phase of a deliverable.

Faculty should expect students to behave like students, not trainees. Their intellectual output builds across time, not in some last-minute rush to the finish line. A consistent pattern of late work is usually a symptom of something else, not students' disregard for the demands of the workplace they hope to enter. Work is often late because faculty did not account for students' failures, flagging self-confidence, or reflection in their pacing of interim project deadlines. Some students successfully hide when they are lost in solving a problem, and their confusion becomes apparent only in the final critique. It is the role of faculty to model a reflective practice in pacing the work of a studio and to coordinate conflicting demands on students' time with colleagues in other courses. Late work is not a problem fixed by punitive policies or scaring students into compliance.

STUDIO PROJECTS AS THE SIGNATURE PEDAGOGY OF DESIGN

Although lecture courses and technical labs appear in the design curricula of most schools, studios are the dominant strategy for developing students' design competencies. Typically composed of fifteen to twenty students and one teacher, these class structures have their origins in the ateliers of the

seventeenth-century École des Beaux-Arts. They are consistent with constructivist views on education in which students bear large responsibility for
their own learning and knowledge is constructed in a social environment.
Today's design studios employ several types of activities, each with different
purposes.

Design exercises ask students to practice or test a particular skill, such as
using software to silhouette an image, joining materials in the shop, or mixing
pigments in progressive changes of color value and saturation. An exercise
tightly constrains activity, producing little variation among student responses.
Faculty generally introduce exercises through demonstrations and evaluate
outcomes under standards of process appropriateness, craftsmanship, or efficiency. Some programs isolate technical skills in discrete courses, building
classroom activities almost entirely around exercises. In other cases, exercises
serve as just-in-time support for projects that have a broader intent.

Exercises can masquerade as more robust projects. There are timeworn
assignments in which faculty-imposed constraints foreshadow likely outcomes before students begin work. In communication design, there is a recurring assignment to design a poster on an historical typeface, arranging three
elements: the name of the typeface, setting of the alphabet, and text describing
the designer. The arrangement strategy conforms to the student's notion of
the style from the period in which the typeface was designed, typically based
on a few visual examples and limited knowledge of the theoretical underpinnings or technological affordances that shaped the style.

Faculty often mistake this project as developing sensitivity to the qualities
of type design or as integrating design history with studio work, when in fact,
it is mostly an exercise in which the intrinsic nature of the three elements
constrains hierarchical relationships. Were students to design two posters with
the intent of varying the hierarchy among the same elements (for example,
compensating for the amount of space occupied by the alphabet by application
of other formal variables), contrasting two typefaces of the same or different
periods in history, or linking the visual qualities of the typeface to technologies of their time, there might be greater educational value. But the scores
of student solutions to this pervasive assignment are literally interchangeable,
raising questions about the depth of learning it presumes to produce.

Design puzzles depend on student discovery of a key principle, which
once identified guides a focused range of successful solutions. There is an
expectation that students will subsequently apply the same principle in other

projects. The classic "egg drop" problem is a design puzzle. Students use a limited inventory of materials (only paper or only toothpicks and glue, for example) to package a raw egg for surviving a long drop to the floor without breaking. Students initially try to solve the problem through an abundance of material, but once they discover the structural properties of triangulation they use a minimum of resources.

Faculty rarely give students clues for solving design puzzles, preferring instead that they discover the principle through experimentation. The evaluative criteria usually appear in the description of the task. For example, the egg drop assignment proclaims a "winner" when the egg survives and the package uses the fewest materials among all successful solutions. The value in a design puzzle increases when followed by projects in which the learned principle is crucial to solving a new problem in a different context—in the case of the egg drop, for example, by a challenge to design portable shelter that uses lightweight materials or a package for shipping glassware. Alone, the puzzle has an *aha!* moment that goes nowhere.

Design projects are individual or collaborative efforts to solve problems or address questions of some consequence in which students are accountable for reconciling competing priorities and choosing among many viable solutions. Design projects are holistic challenges. They are typically long-term activities with real-world implications and link action to some theoretical premise. Design projects have a number of essential characteristics.

Open-endedness

Good design projects arise from questions or challenges that lead to more than one right answer. Although faculty direct students' attention to particular factors and performance outcomes intrinsic to the project, either through an introductory brief or by critique, they are unable to predict the form student solutions will take.

Most faculty acknowledge open-endedness as an essential characteristic of design activity, and it is this quality that often attracts nondesigners to design-based activities as an alternative to the more deterministic scientific method. However, there is a long-held assumption among design faculty that all students in a studio need to be doing roughly the same thing at the same time—that the best learning occurs when students can see how others have solved the same problem. Figure 3.1 illustrates the structure of a communication

FIGURE 3.1 *Leveraging open-endedness.*

Audiences:	Wearing seat belts	Conserving water	Eating a healthy diet	Limiting technology use
Preschool children	1	2	3	4
Non-English speaking adults	5	6	7	8
Teenagers	9	10	11	12
Parents of teenagers	13	14	15	16
Older adults	17	18	19	20

Each of twenty students has a slightly different project defined by a numbered cell in the matrix. The class generates topics that share a persuasive intent, furthering the lesson in how messages change opinion or behavior.

Faculty define different audience types, representing diverse behaviors and attitudes. This contrast in motive focuses student attention of crafting messages with specific characteristics. Both preschoolers and non-English speaking adults have linguistic challenges but the presence of both reveals that an adult reader does not require childish imagery.

Under this structure, students share topic-related and audience-related peers for discussion. They generate solutions that provoke more meaningful understanding of persuasive communication than might arise from work that focuses solely on the form of a single message. And students learn how principles apply to more than content and singular audiences. Not every student needs to be doing the same thing at the same time.

design assignment in which students have slightly different criteria guiding their individual work. Each student has a group of peers that shares the same topic and another that shares the same audience. These groups focus discussions around particular issues, yet the advantage of every student having an individual problem resides in seeing real differences in approach—differences that arise from understanding people and settings, not simply personal judgments about the form that best matches a singular audience and context. The goal in this case is to match the professional demand for designers to transfer concepts and principles from one project context to another, not just to generate several formal solutions to the same problem.

Situatedness

Good design projects describe a context that grounds students' insights and decision-making in the concrete aspects of a real or hypothetical situation. Settings illustrate for students how and where concepts and skills are relevant—"what things are good for"—by applying them under a variety of particular physical, social, cultural, and technological conditions.

It is common in many foundation programs to introduce students to design through abstraction, through problems in the arrangement of two- and three-dimensional shapes lacking both content and context. The assumption is that students must acquire a basic vocabulary of form before later applying it in specific contexts. Typical foundation curricula and textbooks defer discussions of audience, setting, and the construction of meaning until students have mastered this aesthetic language. The problem with this approach is that students generally lack criteria for judging the merits of one abstract composition over another. Most learn these principles by detecting patterns in faculty approval, rather than through comparisons to real interactions with the content-rich, setting-specific world around them. Proponents argue that these principles for formal composition have their origins in basic perceptual behaviors, many as described by Gestalt psychologists at the turn of the twentieth century. However, Gestalt psychology never described these principles in combination, nor did it address the influences of subject matter or context on interpretation.

Designers today return to the work of Russian psychologists from the 1920s for insight into people's need to interact with their surroundings. Lev Vygotsky articulated a theory that reasoning emerges through practical

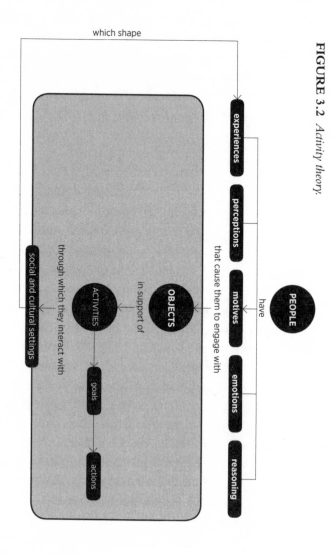

FIGURE 3.2 *Activity theory.*

activity in a social environment and is mediated by signs and symbols. Colleague Aleksie Leontiev furthered Vygotsky's ideas under activity theory, which describes human experience as transactions between people and their physical, social, cultural, and technological settings, driven by fundamental cognitive, emotional, and social motives to engage with others (Figure 3.2). Such beliefs are consistent with current interests in experience design, which view the physical qualities of objects and environments as relevant in engendering certain behaviors and satisfying particular motives. A curriculum composed only of decontextualized, abstract assignments, therefore, overlooks the important mediating purposes of design in today's human-centered practices.

Context, in this sense, provides the framework for explaining designers' choices and judging the qualities of design responses. Architect Christopher Alexander describes design as "the goodness of fit between form and context" (Alexander, 1964). Form is that which designers can shape—including plans, services, and conversations, as well as physical artifacts—and context is the ensemble of factors to which designers fit form. Designers have no control over context other than to determine how much of it to address through form. Consequently, we can judge design not only by its form but also by the designer's ranking of the aspects of context it must address. Projects that avoid any articulation of context rob students of opportunities to make such judgments.

Framing projects in contextual terms does not mean all work must replicate professional assignments. Faculty can foreground aspects of context through project briefs or embed contextual issues in the articulation of project constraints. For example, limiting material options for the design of temporary structures can teach architecture students about sustainability or portability that apply to many different design problems and settings. The point is that a problem without a context or setting isn't really a design problem.

Responsiveness to Someone Other Than the Designer

In addition to being situated in a context, good design projects usually address people's wants and needs beyond those of the designer. They require empathy with an "other" and strategies for learning about what is useful, usable, and desirable for different people.

Today's design practices are human centered in response to an increasingly participatory culture. Many design professionals actively engage people

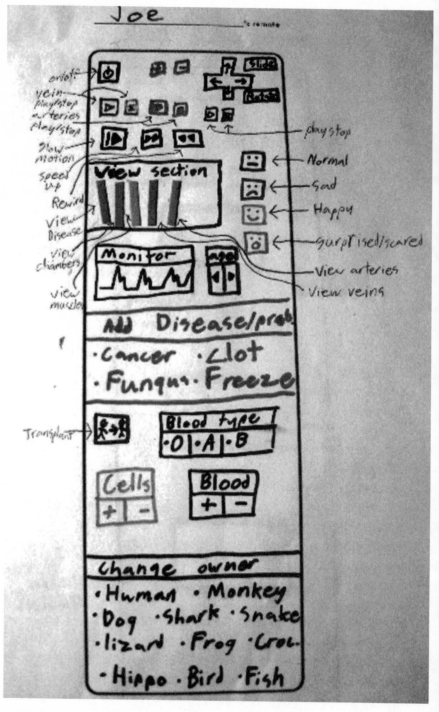

FIGURE 3.3 *A hypothetical remote control designed by grade-seven students for interacting with a program on the anatomy of the human heart.*

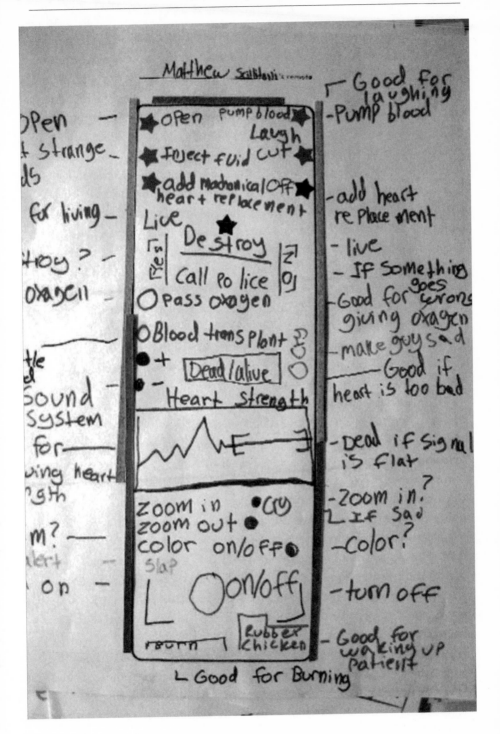

in solving problems. Such collaborators provide input during the design process, ranging from feedback in focus groups to co-creation with a design team.
And many professionals view research about people's behavior, knowledge,
and attitudes as an essential service of their offices.

Graduate student Michelle Wong developed an interactive program to
teach seventh grade students about the nature of the human heart. She might
have asked students a series of questions about the design, but instead she had
them illustrate the functions of a hypothetical remote control device for interacting with the program and its content (Figure 3.3). Students created buttons
that asked the program to "change owner," comparing the human heart to
other species. Another function allowed users to "add a disease," illustrating
the heart under less than optimal performance. It is unlikely these ideas would
have surfaced in a focus group conversation or test of the program in use.

Designers at IDEO, one of the world's largest and most diverse design
firms, argue that solutions to design problems should address the needs of
extreme users, people at the opposite ends of some continuum, such as physical ability, technological savvy, or interest in luxury. In doing so, the needs of
"average" people are more likely to be satisfied than under an approach that
only targets the designer's notion of a typical user.

While architecture and industrial design have a difficult time justify-
ing the absence of implied or explicit users in project briefs, communication design faculty often ignore this aspect of problem-solving in favor of
focusing student attention on the subject matter of messages or describing a
"general" audience with no particular characteristics. Diffusion theories of
communication, however, argue for more nuanced definitions of audience
that go beyond simple demographics. There are people who are not ready
to hear a message; people who are receptive but as yet hold no opinion on
the topic; people who have opinions but are not prepared to act on their
beliefs; and people who are ready to act and advocate for an idea or activity.
The same message is unlikely to be successful with all. So even within a
demographically similar population, there is a continuum of receptivity to
communication on any given content.

Although exercises and puzzles need not designate audiences or users
to be useful in illustrating a concept or principle, design projects that lack
any accountability for someone's experience other than the designer's (even
if the content of that experience is mostly aesthetic) are rarely authentic.
And the further students progress in the curriculum without acknowledging

the beneficiaries of design, the harder it is for them to develop empathy for others and to integrate human-centered values into their problem-solving process.

Values Orientation

It is easy to see how a poster on recycling, potato peeler for people with arthritis, or park pavilion built from reclaimed materials reflect specific values in their problem definitions. In these cases, the intent is to privilege certain user characteristics or aspects of context over others in ways that depart from students' typical conceptions of design as simply making things look good. It is laudable that most faculty see these types of problems as integral to a good design education.

It is just as important, however, for students to understand that all design reflects values and that no design is bias-free. Every design problem requires a ranking of priorities. There is, for example, no more socially oriented design practice than advertising. For better or worse, commercial messages exert much greater influence on the nation's social conscience than save-the-whales or get-out-the-vote posters. It is in how designers satisfy competing constraints—for example, company profit and people's long-term well-being—that designers express social values, not in an either-or consideration of some problems or audiences over others. Project definitions that ignore people and settings conceal the values-oriented nature of designing.

Reverse engineering—extracting knowledge or design information by breaking apart an artifact, environment, plan, or service—reveals to students the designer's weighting of constraints and values that guide decision-making.

The four cups in Figure 3.4, for example, reveal very different designer priorities. The first has a stable shape and retains heat through its small opening and ceramic material. The second is stackable and comfortable to hold with a handle that is convex where the hand is concave and concave where the hand is convex. The third is my grandmother's teacup. The gesture in holding the tiny handle speaks to its role as an object of social use and heritage, but the design sacrifices stability and heat retention to achieve its graceful shape. And the Solo cup is disposable and only suitable for cold liquids. All perform roughly the same function, but it is possible to imagine the settings in which each of the cups might be used and where they might seem out of place.

FIGURE 3.4 *The design of each of these four cups reflects a values-oriented weighting of constraints.*

In this example, form reflects what designers chose to address and what they ignored. Students can also imagine solutions were designers to define the problem more broadly as containing liquid for drinking, rather than a cup: freezer pops, squeeze bottles, juice boxes, and canteens, for example. And an assignment could challenge students to reconcile competing priorities in the design of a fifth cup that is both *stackable and retains heat* or *disposable and elegant*. In other words, any time all possible constraints cannot be satisfied equally well, values play a role in determining which ones receive the most attention in the design.

Integrative

One of the characteristics of design as a practice that is attractive to professionals and educators in nondesign disciplines is its intrinsic interdisciplinarity.

The design process engages whatever expertise necessary to solve a problem. Sometimes that expertise resides in designers; in other cases, it resides in experts from other fields. An architect doesn't look for a mathematician when needing to perform calculations but may consult an engineer on more complex structural issues. An industrial designer doesn't hold a material scientist accountable for selecting the wood for a table but may work with an expert in mass-manufacturing processes related to wood products. As design problems increase in scale beyond those of artifacts, designers require the broader professional knowledge and skills of other fields.

It is not reasonable to ask design education to produce high-level competencies in every relevant discipline, but designers should understand what these fields offer, their characteristic modes of inquiry, and how to read and make use of their research findings in solving design problems. Design projects can send students to other experts, literature, and observations that inform their design work. Discussions in chapter 4 of this book describe the demands of interdisciplinary work and the role of general education in the preparation of a design professional.

Assessable

A good design problem embeds performance criteria in its definition. The design of a package for transporting goldfish from the pet store to home while riding a bicycle implies that conditions for fish survival must be maintained and that the object must account for the physical forces present when pedaling a two-wheel vehicle. The design of a bus shelter suggests that people must be protected from the elements, its form must be distinctive from other structures on the street, and it must not impede pedestrian traffic. In other words, students can infer criteria for success from how faculty frame projects. Definitions leave open the means by which criteria will be met—both a plastic bag and a box for Chinese take-out solve the fish transportation problem for many pet stores—but the students still understand the fundamental conditions for fish survival regardless of the solution.

In other cases, project briefs explicitly state a hierarchy among constraints that guides assessment of student work. For example, if faculty define problem constraints to favor some factors over others, then that should be explicit in the articulation of the design task. When projects are not framed in ways that suggest criteria for judging what separates a "preferred state" from an existing or less desirable one, students either engage in public negotiation of the standards for success (which can be instructive) or spend much of their time seeking individual faculty approval for an acceptable approach. Student comments to faculty such as "Is this what you want?" or "Is this right?" indicate they are not clear regarding what they are to learn from the assignment and the criteria for evaluating their work.

Well-constructed design projects hold students accountable for meeting performance expectations throughout phases of the project, not just in the physical attributes of finished work. For example, if the project brief describes user-centeredness as a high priority, faculty should detect it in students' choices of research methods, inclusion of users in generating possible solutions, testing of prototypes, and comments in critiques.

While good design projects usually exhibit all of these characteristics to some degree, faculty may assign greater weight to a few aspects over others at various times in the semester. For example, an introductory project may be diagnostic in determining where students are in their empathy for users. On the other hand, a final project may seek confirmation that students have developed a personal value system through their conscious ranking of user-centered priorities above other constraints presented by the problem context. Likewise, interim deliverables across the duration of a project may reflect specific aspects of the problem. A concept map may focus on describing the setting for the problem following research, while a three-minute video showing a solution in use may illustrate responsiveness to the people for whom the object is designed.

Chapter 7 of this book offers specific strategies for developing student projects. Although emphasis in the examples is on the application to teaching and learning in nondesign K–12 subjects, these core strategies arise from the history of design education and are suitable for college design classes as well.

SCAFFOLDING

Scaffolding is the construction of a logical sequence of projects or courses in which one learning experience builds on the previous one. Most design faculty scaffold projects and courses from simple to complex or abstract to applied, believing that working with concepts in isolation prepares students for integrating them later in more holistic assignments that account for context and audience. Typography projects, for example, typically begin with the letterform and move through design of the word, paragraph, page, and eventually multi-page publications. Textbooks in the discipline use this progression, and simple-to-complex often distinguishes one typography course from the next in a two- or three-course sequence.

While this typographic scaffolding strategy matched some production processes before the 1980s, today's software asks designers for immediate and simultaneous decisions regarding these differently scaled variables before anything can be made (point size, type weight, line spacing, column width, etc.). It is impossible to address one variable at a time because any conclusions reached in isolation are challenged by variables in combination.

An alternate approach to typographic scaffolding explores the interplay among technological, formal, reading, and language systems, making the point that typography is *relational*—that efforts to define rules of legibility, readability, and expression for all contexts are unlikely to be productive. In this case, a complex-to-simple structure asks students to derive principles from multiple cases, which is more appropriate to the nature of contemporary communication design problems.

There are other organizing principles for scaffolding learning experiences. Efforts to understand different methods or theories suggest a structure of recurring contrast and comparison to overarching concepts or applications. Explorations of participatory culture might order experiences from greater to lesser control of outcomes by designers—from designing artifacts to designing tools and systems through which users create their own products and experiences. Progression through a matrix of interactions among technological, social, cultural, physical, and economic factors might illustrate the interdependent systems that comprise context. The sequence of an audience experience cycle—attracting attention, orienting to use, compelling interaction, and retaining and extending meaning—might define investigations that focus on designing behavior, not objects.

There are many other alternatives to the simple-to-complex or abstract-to-applied scaffolding, but the point is that structure itself contributes to learning. Faculty choices in ordering projects and courses offers students a framework for thinking about design and should arise from articulation of what students should know and be able to do, not from default strategies of the signature pedagogy.

SUMMARY

Lee Shulman's work supports the notion of the studio as the signature pedagogy of design. This approach to teaching and learning can be traced to the
ateliers of the seventeenth century. Consistent with Shulman's observation
that signature pedagogies often outlive their usefulness, however, the current
professional context raises questions regarding the fit between the legacy of
practices in design education and contemporary design challenges.

Design faculty use different types of activities in studio instruction: exercises, puzzles, and projects. Good design projects share some common characteristics. They are open-ended and situated. Students are accountable for
responding to the audience and context and must reconcile competing constraints against some identified value system. The nature of work in design is
by definition integrative of skills and knowledge from a variety of fields and
can be assessed through performance criteria that are implicit or explicit in
the problem definition.

Scaffolding is a deliberate sequencing of projects or courses that reflects
overarching principles and frames how students think about curricular content. The signature pedagogy typically scaffolds projects and courses from simple to complex or abstract to applied, but there are other alternatives that
appear better matched to contemporary demands of practice.

CHAPTER 4:
INTERDISCIPLINARITY AND TEACHING
COLLABORATION IN DESIGN

I attended a conference at which a faculty panel cited students' low opinions of group work. I asked panelists if they prepared students specifically for collaboration and assessed their individual effectiveness as group members. None provided instruction, and all awarded students in the group the same grade. It is difficult to imagine students valuing participation with others if faculty behavior suggests it is less important than other learning tasks.

There is little debate over the current need to collaborate across disciplines. Many of today's problems are too big and too consequential to be solved by an individual or even a single field of expertise. They require teamwork among designers and between designers and professionals in other disciplines.

Disciplines have tools, methods, and theories that reflect characteristic worldviews. The values that underpin these perspectives allow professionals to distinguish good work from bad and experts from novices (Klein, 1990). Worldviews and their corresponding questions change at particular times in disciplinary histories. Some disciplines remain close to their origins; others evolve, responding to modulations in the surrounding culture and borrowing freely from other fields. Once concerned with the attributes of messages, many communication designers today focus on the experiences of users. Over the last decades, their collaborators shifted from typesetters and photographers to technologists, cognitive psychologists, and ethnographers. The challenge in these new interdisciplinary collaborations is to understand how participating partners view the problem and the questions that drive their decision-making.

The terminology that describes how disciplines and practices work together can be confusing. Multi-, cross-, trans-, and interdisciplinary are often used interchangeably to describe practices that involve more than one field; however, there are distinctions among the ways in which fields collaborate in solving design problems. In some cases, collaboration among disciplines represents a division of labor, with each field executing its respective responsibilities under a clear hierarchy of control in decision-making. For example, a social scientist may deliver an ethnographic study to a design team without further engagement in the project. An industrial designer may develop products that are part of a larger innovation strategy in business but not have much to say about the service ecology that supports those products. In other collaborative strategies, teams of disciplinary experts work under flat hierarchies in which various fields contribute equally to most aspects of a project. In these instances, good ideas come from anywhere and flourish under a working structure that celebrates disciplinary differences. Yet other investigations transfer the methods or theories of one discipline to the practices of another, as in the current interest by business in design thinking. In all cases, the intent is to work beyond the boundaries of a single field and to benefit from alternate perspectives that shift traditional views on problems.

A BRIEF HISTORY OF INTERDISCIPLINARITY

Aspirations to work across fields are not new. They can be found in the writings of ancient philosophers and throughout history. The explicit organization of college curricula for the integration of knowledge across disciplines has been a preoccupation of universities since the nineteenth century, when the nature of work brought about by the Industrial Revolution and advances in technology and science pressured institutions to specialize undergraduate education (Klein, 1990). The result was the compartmentalization of scholarship into a new academic landscape of discrete majors and departments (Menand, 2010).

After decades of this specialization, twentieth-century academics feared that a well-rounded education was not possible under narrowly defined fields of study. Ernest Boyer, president of the Carnegie Foundation for the Advancement of Teaching from 1979 to 1995, described the movement to educate the "whole person" as a response to the misplaced vocational emphasis of institutions, as well as the need for a national sense of unity amidst political and social turmoil in the early decades of the twentieth century (Boyer, 1981). Harvard, Columbia, and the University of Chicago led the way by instituting a *general education* core curriculum for undergraduates to remedy the problem. Originally built around great ideas and books of Western civilization, the content of these course groupings included the humanities and social sciences to ensure that college curricula expressed the values of an educated world (Klein, 1990).

Area studies appeared as an approach in the late 1930s, predicated on a belief in comprehensive integrated knowledge. A "doctrine of concentration" argued, "the mind advances when wholly immersed in one interest but connections [are] made with related subjects" (Klein, 1990, p. 27). Universities restructured fields around theoretical perspectives regarding what disciplines had in common, spawning new areas of scholarship and methods of inquiry such as cultural geography and behavioral sciences (Klein, 1990).

By the last half of the twentieth century, however, financial incentives motivated universities to tackle the practical problems of government and industry that were not being addressed by traditional fields of study (Klein, 1990). There was a desire to establish distinct institutional identities for working across fields in an effort to attract outside funding. This growing focus on funded interdisciplinary research was matched by student interest in solving real-world problems and making connections across disciplines as way of developing critical and creative thinking skills.

As a result of this history, today's college curricula face the dual mission of providing a strong general education and also preparing students for future employment in emerging fields valued by a knowledge economy. Ironically, these new specializations are often hybrids—bioengineering and informatics, for example—that initially relied on experts from different disciplines in their formation. Therefore, the current pressure for interdisciplinary activity in colleges and universities has both philosophical and practical origins (Klein, 1990, p. 42).

To some extent, studies in modern design practices owe their development to interdisciplinary interests. In many European institutions and a few schools in the United States, broad studies in design supported a primary specialization. Architecture was often seen as the "mother discipline," with graduates working in all design fields after completion of their studies. Graphic design at NC State University, for example, was seen as a basic skill set—not a major—that supported study in architecture, landscape architecture, and industrial design well into the 1980s. In other cases, design study originated in departments or colleges not designated as "design." A number of architecture and industrial design programs trace their origins to engineering colleges. Interior design programs typically emerged as concentrations in home economics curricula. And communication design programs were frequently located in art departments. In many instances, these original locations no longer serve program missions or evolving professions. There have been recent university efforts to consolidate study under multidisciplinary schools of design or to form new alliances with nondesign disciplines, such as business, engineering, and mass communications.

Interdisciplinary student projects of the 1970s often stratified responsibilities among various design majors: architects designed buildings, industrial designers designed furniture, and communication designers designed signage and presentations under collaborative investigations. Rarely did these projects question differing disciplinary perspectives—asking, for example, how architecture might be framed as a communication problem or how products extend brand identity. Some design programs worked with other disciplines in the same academic unit—graphic designers and artists on catalog and book arts projects, industrial designers and engineers on sponsored product development with industry, and architects and planners on community development. Such partnerships typically involved adjacent disciplines and a clear division of labor, rather than fields that might challenge traditional views of design problems and processes.

A second variation of interdisciplinary design activity in the 1970s involved the study of methods and design thinking. William Peña's *Problem Seeking*, Chris Jones' *Design Methods*, Christopher Alexander's *Pattern Language*, Don Koberg's *Universal Traveler*, Kevin Lynch's *Image of the City*, Lawrence Halprin's *RSVP Cycles*, and Charles Owens' *Design Process Newsletters* focused attention on analytical strategies that appeared applicable across design fields (Davis, 2015). All originated in ideas from architectural programming and engineering. The intent was to formulate a systematic, "glass box" approach to better address complex problems and to distinguish design practice from more intuitive work in fine art, a mission advocated by the interdisciplinary planning and "science of design" emphasis at the Ulm School of Design in the 1950s and 1960s. British researchers Bruce Archer, Bryan Lawson, and Nigel Cross provided some of the earliest writing on design thinking and methods but also framed studies in terms of architectural and engineering education.

Things changed in the 1980s and 1990s, driven again by both philosophical and practical interests. Postmodern critical writing of the 1970s found receptive audiences among architects, designers, and academics, who looked for a subjective, pluralistic approach to design after decades of late modernist, International Style neutrality. Designers and architects sought inspiration in texts from the fields of literary criticism, cultural and social theory, linguistics, philosophy, and media studies. Professional work served the role of commenting on culture as well as solving functional problems. Academic collaborations were often between designers and writers, philosophers, and critics (Figure 4.1), and faculty encouraged students to discover writing in the humanities as motivation for design form.

Cranbrook Academy of Art, for example, explored the cultural semantics of products and communication. Students rejected what they saw as the prescriptive syntactical interests of late modernism in favor of ideas that assigned the construction of meaning to audiences rather than the designer. In architecture, postmodern ideas reinvigorated interest in the study of architectural history as a source for the critical repurposing of form and explanation of broader ideas regarding the relationship between design and culture. MIT, Cornell, Princeton, Berkeley, and Columbia in the United States established doctoral programs in architectural history to distinguish themselves from PhD programs in art history, which showed less concern for popular culture and the influence of context on interpretation. In other fields, new synthetic perspectives emerged, such as information theory, cultural theory, and visual rhetoric.

While cross-cutting design theories grew in importance, digital technology simultaneously transformed the practical work of the design professions and college curricula. Software collapsed the generation of form and technical production in industrial and graphic design, reorganizing workflow and challenging traditional ideas about craft, entry-level qualifications for young designers, and the content and nature of collaboration. In architecture and interior design, CAD systems and Building Information Modeling (BIM) raised similar questions about traditional practices, although with less effect on the ideational phases of the design process.

In 1998 under the leadership of Clement Mok, the AIGA formed the Advance for Design to define and build an interdisciplinary community of practitioners who would "shape and advocate for the role of design in a world that is increasingly digital" (AIGA in Malone, 2002). Designers, design educators, business executives, software and technology developers,

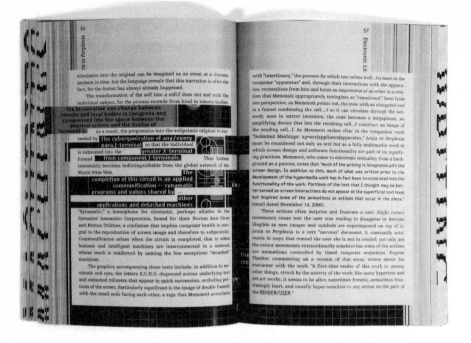

FIGURE 4.1 *Writing Machines was a collaboration between Duke University writing professor Katherine Hayles and Art Center College of Design graphic designer Anne Burdick. Tracing a journey from the 1950s through the 1990s, Hayles uses the autobiographical persona of Kaye to explore how literature has transformed itself from inscriptions rendered as the flat durable marks of print to the dynamic images of CRT screens, from verbal texts to the diverse sensory modalities of multimedia works, from books to technotexts (MIT Press).*

and human factors experts met over several summers for discourse about the challenges in advancing the interdisciplinary practice of *experience design*. Among the self-initiated tasks was to publish guidelines for study in college design programs. The consensus at the time was that the practice was best left to those with advanced degrees, but the group did identify principles that would prepare undergraduates to work as members of interdisciplinary design teams:

- Influencing designed user experiences through more than the visual attributes of communication, products, and environments;
- Viewing users' interactions with designed objects, environments, and services across entire lifecycles, from the users' identification of needs

or desires to when they discard the object, abandon the environment, or discontinue the service;

- Creating relationships between experiences and individuals, not mass markets;
- Invoking and creating communication, products, and environments that connect with users emotionally and in terms of added valued; and
- Building upon the traditional design disciplines but also exploring new collaborations with nondesigners, such as experts in computer programming, human factors, cognitive science, business, etc. (Davis et al, 2002).

Other important issues called for collaboration among fields of study. Urgency in addressing the effects of climate change and resource depletion; globalization in the design, production, and distribution of products; and growing concern for social innovation highlighted the need for disciplines to work together. These issues set the agenda for a number of innovative graduate programs that today encourage enrollment by students whose first degrees are not in design. Faculty from a variety of disciplinary backgrounds mirror the student populations in these programs and conduct research in areas not traditionally associated with studio-based design practices.

While college-level design programs today acknowledge the importance of collaboration, there are barriers to effective interdisciplinary work. Increasing reliance on student-owned technology (or use of common computer labs) and competition for studio space in high enrollment design programs have transformed some classrooms from active working environments to critique spaces where students simply "check in" for feedback. Used to relying on digital connections to everything and distracted by the necessity of off-campus employment, many students are impatient with any work that requires them to be on campus. Therefore, faculty need to rebuild students' appreciation for the value of colleagues in the design process by providing workspaces that are significantly different from those of the past and leveraging technology in new types of collaboration.

Most studio spaces are designed for individual, artifact-driven work and one-on-one desk critiques as the dominant teaching strategy. A number of institutions have explored alternatives, developing temporary collaborative project spaces with floor-to-ceiling white boards, flat-screen monitors that display work from student-owned computers, and furniture that can be reconfigured to match the needs of teams. In other cases, networked technology supports collaboration.

A counting-and-measuring culture in many schools also presents challenges to teaching across fields. How are class schedules aligned in ways that make it possible for diverse student groups to work together? Which program receives credit for the teaching assignment, and how are faculty teaching loads determined? How do faculty prepare to work across fields? Do tenure and promotion committees have positive views on faculty departure from traditional lines of inquiry? How do programs commit resources on a continuing basis that makes collaboration a predictable feature of the curriculum? Clearly, interdisciplinary work calls into question the signature pedagogy of design and how new kinds of work will be accommodated in the future.

TEACHING COLLABORATION

It is easy to assume that today's design students are more experienced in collaboration than any previous generation. They have participated in organized group activities since childhood and live through social media that involve constant interaction with peers. These early activities, however, rarely depend on developing leadership skills—every child receives an award for simply showing up—and Facebook conversation is a long way from the high-stakes, face-to-face negotiation of strategy in graded college assignments. In fact, a highly structured childhood and technologically mediated social interaction may actually work against college students' adaptive responses to alternate worldviews and the development of interpersonal skills necessary for collaboration.

Although design professionals often show better-than-average skills at working in groups, there is little evidence that faculty actually teach design students how to collaborate. As the previous history illustrates, much group work in design programs has been with design classmates who share terminology, methods, and values or with clients in which the designer is clearly the expert in charge. It is not surprising, therefore, that many design students express aversion to group work that distributes responsibility for outcomes beyond their individual control. They describe uneven contributions to work by group members, clashes of ego and perspectives, and work that doesn't meet their personal standards as frequent outcomes of collaborative projects.

While design faculty voice commitment to preparing students for team-work, few structure activities specifically for learning how to work with others. Typically, the three-heads-better-than-one justification is about generating multiple solutions to a problem through brainstorming, not about the quality of the collaborative experience it takes to produce effective work throughout the design process.

Students also value performances that are assessed by faculty. Like it or not, grades are the currency through which students judge the value of educational experiences. So if faculty don't evaluate the quality of students' collaboration—or leave evaluation to their student partners, the very people in whom they have the least trust for objectivity—the ultimate message is that the effectiveness of social interaction in solving problems holds little importance in their professional development. Avoiding confrontation and separating a discrete task over which to exercise individual control often become students' first priorities in group work.

There are activities that can prepare students for collaboration.

- Figure 4.2 itemizes a number of behaviors that participants are likely to exhibit in collaborative work. There are more and faculty can customize any list, but it is important to limit the list to what students can observe and quickly inventory. The activity asks one group of students to solve an assigned problem and a second group to observe their interactions, assessing peers through an undisclosed list of behaviors. Each observing group member watches an individual designer as he/she participates in analyzing and generating a solution to the assigned problem, adding a mark to the inventory each time the designer exhibits a particular behavior. At the conclusion of the activity, observers privately share their analyses with designers, identifying interpersonal characteristics that engage and encourage fellow collaborators, reinforce good ideas, and assist in reaching conclusions. The activity also reveals negative behaviors that shut down conversation or disparage contributions by others. It teaches students that their individual conduct has something to do with the quality of outcomes.
- A second activity establishes the same observer/designer relationship and maps patterns of discussion between the person being observed and other participants in the group. Using arrows to indicate the direction of comments on a seating chart for the group, observers

FIGURE 4.2 *Observation of collaborative behavior.*

Seeks opinions from another team member	_____
Asks questions or seeks clarification from another team member	_____
Offers suggestions	_____
Tags onto or praises someone else's ideas	_____
Defends another team member	_____
Proposes ways to move teamwork forward	_____
Restates the status of the project at the start or end of the meeting	_____
Builds consensus among group members who disagree	_____
Interrupts another team member	_____
Changes the subject of conversation	_____
Criticizes or makes fun of someone else's idea	_____
Ignores the comment or suggestion of another team member	_____
Makes negative gestures or facial expressions	_____
Escalates disagreements into arguments	_____
Disengages from group activity or conversation	_____
Works on a parallel problem to the work of the team	_____
Engages in an "aside" conversation with another team member or suggests splitting the group effort	_____

mark the intended recipient(s) of remarks made by a participant. The activity reveals who is active and who is passive in the discussion, as well as individuals who tend to dominate conversation or are seen by the group as a leader. Further, it illustrates the effect of seating arrangements on group interactions. Individuals sitting at the corners of tables, for example, have greater difficulty entering the conversation than those in the center. And when two dominant personalities sit opposite each other, they often represent a shortcut for dialogue that disengages those to their left and right. This activity suggests to students that the physical arrangement of their workspace matters.

- Although conflict is often a sign of healthy interaction and intellectual investment among members of a group, it can be paralyzing if not eventually resolved. Faculty can prepare students for this likelihood by requiring them to follow several protocols for group work:

  - *Articulating workflow*: Students are notoriously optimistic about their ability to complete work in compressed periods of time. As a result, they often defer action for too long and find themselves making critical decisions under pressure and executing work at the last minute without opportunities for reflection and discussion. In some cases, students spend too much debating an issue without playing out the consequences of alternatives through action. Requiring students to identify the steps in their process and to allocate time for each step prepares them for project work and develops skills necessary for group work in the field. Faculty can monitor and evaluate student progress in managing time as one component of team performance.

  - *Negotiating decision-making criteria before beginning work*: Students may decide that a majority vote based on articulated pluses and minuses of alternatives, for example, will resolve disagreement. Or they may ask for an external recommendation from several classmates outside the group. The goal is to decide on a strategy for resolving conflict before it occurs and agree to move forward with conclusions once a decision is made. In the case of complex tasks, negotiating the criteria for making judgments among alternatives is also important. For example, students may decide that breadth is more important than depth in a research task or that the number of ideas is more important than refinement of individual solutions in the early stages of a project. Conflict often arises within groups when criteria for making decisions are not public and negotiated.

  - *Developing a way to archive decision-making*: Technology can assist students in tracking their decision-making. If students end each session by archiving decisions made, identifying assignments to be completed, and describing the purpose and content of the next meeting, there will be greater likelihood of regular progress. Many group meltdowns occur because students proceed without consensus or disagree on what they decided, placing them

behind in meeting project expectations. Faculty can ask students
to defer decisions from one meeting to the start of the next in
order to reflect on possible outcomes. This forestalls knee-jerk
responses and entrenched positions that often escalate in full-
blown conflict.

- *Sharing leadership responsibilities*: Developing leadership skills is an
  important goal of collaboration, yet students are often unwill-
  ing to direct the work of a team for fear of alienating peers or
  carrying the burden of success or failure in a graded assignment.
  By deliberately rotating responsibility for leading each session
  among group members, faculty relieve students from the interpersonal outcomes of "taking charge" and teach project management skills. A brief meeting among group leaders after a work
  session can evaluate leadership approaches that did and did not
  go as planned.

- Because students generally have difficult histories of collaboration,
  a pedagogical strategy that eases them into the process of working
  together is useful. For example, starting group work with the low-
  stakes activity of research helps students build trust. Research rarely
  involves either/or decisions. Assigning specific research methods gives
  students practice in organizing work that has clear protocols to follow. Bruce Hanington's book *Universal Methods of Design: 100 Ways to
  Research Complex Problems* provides coherent explanations of research
  methods that can guide student work while they learn how to collaborate.

- Group fatigue also undermines successful collaboration. When students are too familiar with the same group members from activity
  to activity or critique to critique, they ask fewer questions of each
  other and pay less attention to their behavior as collaborators. Faculty
  can divide groups for discussions, clustering members from various
  groups for feedback at different times in the project trajectory. One
  member from each group reporting to others requires reflection on
  the status of the project and yields fresh insights.

There are many other ways to structure group activities, but it is important
for faculty to identify what it is about group work they intend to teach and
evaluate. Rarely can students be left on their own to acquire these skills.

GENERAL EDUCATION AND STUDY IN DESIGN

As discussed earlier, the history of interdisciplinarity includes forces that argue for both specialization and a well-rounded education. The concept of general education was developed to balance the narrow view of immersion in a discipline with broad exposure to diverse modes of inquiry. Typically, students select general education courses from approved lists of offerings in the humanities, social sciences, and basic sciences. The breadth of these lists and depth of faculty resources depend on the institution, but there are usually more options in universities than in single discipline art schools. A university committee typically reviews courses for inclusion in general education lists.

In most architecture and design programs, enrollment in general education coursework is concurrent with design study, unless students transfer from two-year institutions where they completed nondesign requirements. Despite this simultaneous registration, the curricular relationship between design study and general education is usually one of *proximity* rather than *integration*. Design faculty rarely provide perspectives or expertise in general education content and make little use of it in design projects.

In some schools, liberal arts faculty try to narrow the gap between study inside and outside the design major by delivering instruction to classes composed entirely of art and design majors and by customizing assignments to their specific interests. While this appears to accommodate students' learning preferences, external curriculum reviewers frequently hear student complaints regarding this approach. Students clearly prefer design courses to other classes—both in content and instructional style—but they also recognize the contribution general education makes to their intellectual life as professionals. Naturally curious, many have secondary interests outside of design. To some extent, students believe that faculty underestimate their capacity for learning in nondesign classes and resent lowered standards.

Under other proximity relationships, general education content enters the design curriculum as the topical subject matter of projects otherwise focused on a design principle. For example, a communication design assignment to explain scientific phenomena may require students to research theories of evolution or what causes lightning. In such projects, however, the scientific information is neither integral to the design principle nor fundamental to a method that is generalizable in other contexts. Alternative content—photosynthesis, for example—could be equally effective in achieving the outcomes of the project. Design faculty rarely check content accuracy or debate students' choices of topics from a larger body of information. Appropriateness has more to do with affordances for particular types of communicative form—for example, diagrams or visual explanations of invisible processes—than with applicability to design theory or strategy (Davis et al., 2004).

Architecture curricula address issues of math and science related to structures and environmental systems as part of the design curriculum but often in discrete courses under faculty responsible solely for such specialized instruction. Some students complain that studio faculty pay little attention to structural details or energy conservation, expressing concern that they are left on their own to understand the application of these concepts in a first job.

In relationships of *integration*, design faculty refer to general education content specifically for its relevance to the outcomes of design and issues that transcend individual projects or formats. The role of design faculty is to make explicit how such information from other disciplines informs students' decision-making. In these classrooms, form is frequently evaluated in terms of its consequences in larger systems that are not visual or spatial. For example, an assignment to design affordable housing can nest design decisions within study of complex cultural and economic systems. In teaching design history, many faculty find it necessary to draw on content from outside the discipline. It is easy to see how art history or social history might contribute to students' understanding of design milestones, but faculty are less likely to cite histories of technology and economics.

Design students also need experience in interpreting the design implications of research findings in other fields: ethnographies that use thick description, sociological studies that identify social patterns and trajectories, and engineering tests that calculate structural integrity. Designers cannot assume that the strategies they use to address problems are interchangeable with modes of inquiry in other fields. This is important content if students are to be effective in interdisciplinary work, but understanding these disciplinary differences requires explicit discussions regarding how fields do their work and the value systems that drive questions.

THE EDUCATION OF THE DESIGN GENERALIST

One frequent argument in the discourse on disciplinary specialization is that today's students are likely to have as many as seven careers in their lifetimes and that a broad education prepares them for changes in employment. A study by the *Wall Street Journal*, however, could find no source for these statistics, despite many articles that inaccurately attributed them to the US Bureau of Labor Statistics (Bialik, 2010). The newspaper found that most employment changes happen between the ages of sixteen and twenty-four as students test their interests and fund their education through short-term jobs. It further determined that adults who advance in their fields technically change jobs but really take on greater responsibilities within the same profession. The paper also suggested probable distortion in claims of frequent job changes because reports come from career specialists who deal only with people seeking new employment. In fact, the US Bureau of Labor Statistics reported that people's employment patterns have been relatively stable (Bialik, 2010).

What should matter to educators is why students' change disciplinary directions and how they apply learning across professional boundaries. Does sampling coursework in a variety of fields develop a broad set of interests that cannot be assigned to a single discipline? Or do students learn through focused study a particular way of seeing the world that makes them assets outside their original field? Or do accomplished people who understand something deeply naturally pursue other interests to explore what they know in different contexts? It is probably all of these things. Most faculty can name individuals who succeed under each approach to learning. But how do colleges and universities build curricula that best meet the educational goals of most students, while also preparing students who choose not to live and work within one field of practice (Davis, 2015)?

A generalist knows something about a lot of things. The general practitioner in medicine, for example, focuses on overall wellness as much as illness, on the whole person and health across a lifetime. He doesn't perform major surgery or advise on cancer treatments. There are some very specific things to learn about being a generalist. In medicine, there is agreement in the field regarding the educational path to becoming a generalist. There are journals and conferences, continuing education, protocols for working with patients, and standards of practice. Therefore, the education of the general practitioner in medicine is shaped by more than random courses or the first two years of a specialty. And it is understood that a premed curriculum is not enough, that an advanced degree is required to understand the content of general practice (Davis, 2015).

The student's choice of an institution and degree type is the first commitment to specialized versus general study in design. Professional degree programs require significantly higher percentages of coursework in the major than do liberal arts or preprofessional degrees. If the promotional materials of a college program and its faculty advisors fail to distinguish the outcomes of liberal arts study in design from those of a professional degree, students are rightfully confused. They often learn of the differences too late in their education. Graduate program directors report many applicants return to school because they lack the job qualifications for practice promised by their bachelor's study. Truth in advertising calls for faculty to embrace what is possible under the number of available credits in design and to communicate it accurately to prospective students.

Some institutions offer both specialized and general degree programs. Students who are undecided about a specialized major appropriately choose the liberal arts degree as a way of acquiring an overview of design issues. Unfortunately, other institutions use the BA/BS as a default practice-oriented program for students who are unsuccessful in mid-program reviews for admission to professional degrees. This strategy creates perceptions of a "second class" degree or confuses all students that there is a shorter path to the same outcomes as the professional program. Introductory courses in professional degree programs rarely address a generalist mission, nor are they adequate preparation for practice. It is not enough, therefore, to define a general education in design as "professional lite."

Design generalists have a role to play in collaborative work. When prepared by their curricular experiences, they can expose the limitations of conventional modes of inquiry; translate concepts that are otherwise constrained by disciplinary jargon and methods of representation; position strategies within broader contexts than the immediate assignment; and identify intellectual resources that may be outside the experience of specialists (Davis, 2015). Like the general practitioner in medicine, they can provide an overview of issues and coordinate the implementation of recommendations by specialists.

General curricula, however, must be designed and not left to chance or constructed entirely from bits and pieces of coursework that serve entirely different purposes for discrete professional degrees (Davis, 2015). Scholar James Elkins admonishes visual studies programs—a parallel to the more recent design studies offerings—to become "more ambitious about its purview, more demanding in its analysis, and above all more difficult" (Elkins, 2003, p. vii).

INCREASING DEMANDS OF INTERDISCIPLINARY
PRACTICE ON GRADUATE EDUCATION

Many of the preceding discussions in this book address baccalaureate study that prepares students for practice in a design field. It is common for students entering communication design majors, for example, to describe magazine or web design as primary interests because it is what they know as users. Across four or more years of undergraduate study, most expand their understanding of the field and discover personal aptitudes and interests in particular kinds of work. Others view their design education simply as grounding for later work in another field.

In contrast, applicants to graduate programs typically know more about their respective design fields and have preferences for the type of work they hope to undertake (or conversely, hope to avoid). Many choose institutions for the program emphasis, faculty perspectives and reputations, and institutional resources. Others seek mentoring relationships with faculty as preparation for teaching careers or aspire to hybrid practices that integrate their graduate work in design with previous study in another discipline.

The traditional intent of graduate education has been the refinement of skills and insights in the crafting of messages, objects, and environments. Compared to other fields, graduate design programs are relatively recent additions to college offerings. Most borrow their curricular practices from advanced study in fine arts: admission criteria weighted in favor of portfolio evidence; largely self-directed work across two or more years of studio-based study; and a culminating exhibition or demonstration project that determines graduation. While these traditions seemed appropriate to an artifact-driven design culture, they fall short in reflecting new demands for interdisciplinary work on problems of greater scale and complexity than artifacts, the design of systems upon which others build solutions, and design research that generates new knowledge for the field.

Some argue that crafting artifacts will always be a role for design, and admittedly, *smart* is not the opposite of *beautiful*. But in the face of rapid growth in the number of new graduate design programs in the United States, the design fields should ask several important questions. How many artifact-centered programs does the nation need, given the size of the design professions and cost of a college education? What does graduate education offer to craft-based work that cannot be developed through a strong undergraduate education and professional experience? And who will take on the interdisciplinary agenda in design if not institutions that offer advanced study?

There are incentives for institutions to develop advanced degree programs. State legislatures fund graduate enrollment at higher rates than undergraduate enrollment, faculty perceive graduate offerings as status within and among institutions, and graduate students provide cheap labor as teaching and research assistants in understaffed programs. Design departments frequently launch graduate study with no additional faculty, teaching students largely through independent study or in piggybacked courses with undergraduates. In schools where the number of design applicants fail to achieve critical mass, students may be admitted under a broadly defined MFA with fine artists. Their seminars address issues of general interest in the arts, rather than the pressing concerns of the design fields. Although there are a few notable examples of curricular emphases in areas of emerging design issues, most contemporary master's programs reinforce a traditional model of practice. They may include work in a new medium or broaden requirements to include other skills—for example, in interaction design or writing—but the curricular structure of graduate programs in design has remained largely unchanged over the last five decades.

If the continuing relevance of design depends on responding to shifting conditions in the twenty-first century context for practice, then graduate programs must change. Professional master's programs must define a more ambitious agenda than one of linear processes in pursuit of stable constraints. Advanced study must address the interdependency of variables in large-scale systems and the parallel need to collaborate with other fields. And it must build respect for the value of research and what design can learn from more mature disciplines.

Although bringing about curricular change is crucial for repositioning design as more than making things look good and work better, or cheerleading for creativity in business, a greater argument for new graduate missions is the impact on undergraduate education. Master's students in design represent the next generation of the professoriate, and they teach what they studied. If their graduate curricula reinforce traditional views of practice, then that is what alumni are prepared to teach. Graduate study also shapes design faculty views of what is appropriate as research and enables or constrains the ability to work with experts in other fields.

While master's programs have remained largely unchanged across the last half-century, the development of doctoral study in design in the United

States is promising for addressing an interdisciplinary research agenda. Unlike Europe where there is equivocation on what defines doctoral study, existing PhD design programs in the United States appear to agree that the focus is research, not studio-based professional practice. Doctoral study in architecture has a longer history than in other design disciplines, but it is significant that four programs in the United States that accept students with backgrounds in graphic and industrial design (Illinois Institute of Technology, NC State University, Carnegie Mellon University, and Arizona State University) are interdisciplinary in their research interests and involve faculty from outside the design disciplines. Further, all teach research methods that have their origins in the social sciences with the intent of customizing them to fit the particular needs of design research. Although small in number, graduates of these programs have increasing influence on campuses and in the profession.

The challenge in doctoral education is to define *what is worth doing* among the plethora of pressing research issues in the field. Largely educated in studio-based master's programs, novice researchers receive mixed messages from the field. A 2005 survey by *Metropolis Magazine* asked 1,051 design professionals, faculty, and students about design research topics (Manfra, 2005). Although generally confused regarding a definition of design research, respondents ranked *sustainability* as the number one priority. At the same time, *systems theory* was at the bottom of their lists of important research content. It is difficult to research sustainable solutions to design problems without an understanding of systems. *Technology* ranked near the top of respondents' lists, but *computer science* was near the bottom. And many favored *culture* as the content of future research but ranked work in *anthropology* much lower than other subjects. Admittedly, this was not a scholarly audience with formal training in research, but it was a reflection of general understanding in the field regarding the scope and interdisciplinary nature of contemporary problems.

College faculty are equally confused about their institutional obligations for research. To establish legitimacy in universities dominated by an established scientific research culture, design faculty struggle to frame research in ways that are both rigorous in meeting the standards of research collaborators in other fields and authentic to design.

I have reviewed more than seventy faculty research dossiers. A collection of faculty publications compared the speed of recognition of Cook and Shanosky's 1974 pictographic travel symbols by readers of ideographic and phonetic languages. The sample size was much too small to be generalizable, and the differences in recognition by the two audiences were negligible. More confusing, however, was what the researcher thought the findings of this published study meant for the design of symbol systems, global communication, or research in the cognitive processing of visual phenomena. In what way was recognition of these symbols meaningful outside of their contextual environment? Under what theory was recognition proved attributable to their native languages? How could researchers assume that subjects were "innocent" of these pictographic systems prior to testing? And in today's global travel environment, where is it possible to separate readers of ideographic and phonetic languages? In other words, the study suffered under the rigorous criteria of social science research and the context for application by design professionals.

University of Colorado/Boulder professor Rick Robinson, who pioneered design research methods at E-Lab and Iota Partners (now Sapient), affirmed growing accountability for rigor and interdisciplinary engagement in design research.

> Research needs to be justified on an ongoing, long-term basis, not purely on a 'see what we found!' case-by-case basis. . . . There are very few design issues that are understood as stand-alone problems today. Contexts are connected and dependencies are everywhere. A systems-level view of the world dominates the way organizations understand what needs to be designed. Scaling design research beyond one-off projects means building an ecosystem of providers and processes, of institutionalizing the research work while remaining open to change (Robinson, 2016).

The nascent research culture in design has much to learn from other fields that have longer histories in the academy and the generation of new knowledge. It is time to look outside the arts for models of graduate education and to challenge the "normal science" of design that continues to apply artifact-centered principles to problems of greater scope and less clarity.

SUMMARY

The history of interdisciplinary activity versus specialization illustrates the need to sort out curricular strategies for preparing students for contemporary practice. Simple collaborations among different types of designers and leaving students to resolve inevitable conflicts in group work are no longer effective approaches to the complexity of today's problems. As Donald Norman cautions, the principles for solving complex problems bear little resemblance to those through which most of today's design faculty prepared for professional practice (see chapter 1). Interdisciplinarity is a struggle to reconcile a system that demands and supports specialization with a concurrent need for expanded views of problems and their solutions (Davis, 2015). Critic Louis Menand describes professors in "a real fight, a fight not with each other and our schools . . . but with the forces that make and remake the world most human beings live in" (Menand, 2010, p. 125).

CHAPTER 5:
ASSESSING STUDENT AND
CURRICULAR PERFORMANCE

Among the most frequent complaints I read in student evaluations of faculty during my years in administration were that faculty changed the "rules of the game" across the duration of a project and grades did not appropriately reflect differences in students' performance. Students also resented hearing about shortfalls in their work for the first time in final critiques. It was unclear whether these comments accurately described faculty behavior, but it was evident that students were confused about expectations and outcomes.

EVALUATING CREATIVITY

Current use of the terms "creativity," "innovation," and "design thinking" can be perplexing to design students. They have been praised as being "creative" for cliché paintings of sailboats and palm trees or the arrangement of photographs on a printer's grid in high school yearbooks. Advertising tells them that Cindy Crawford's history as a supermodel qualifies her as a furniture designer. And business leaders argue that design thinking, now deemed essential to innovation, can be left to people with MBAs. In other words, students enter college from a culture with little understanding of what these concepts and the standards for judging them really mean.

Faculty are responsible for assessing an array of students' critical and creative thinking behaviors. They need observable evidence that student performance meets some appropriate threshold for the assigned task and is consistent with the future demands of professional practice. Criticism must be constructive and specific to inform future action. Most design faculty evaluate students through artifacts—physical objects presumed to embody students' understanding of constraints and opportunities and evidence of originality. Research, however, cautions against reducing the assessment of critical and creative thinking to this limited form of evidence.

Psychologist Mihaly Csikszentmihalyi describes the creative person as someone who changes an aspect of culture or establishes a new domain, not someone who simply expresses eccentric thoughts or sees the world in novel ways (Csikszentmihalyi, 1996). He qualifies creativity as composed of: a domain with a set of symbolic rules and procedures that are shared within a culture; a field (teachers, critics, curators, practitioners) that decides whether new ideas should be included in the domain; and an individual who uses the symbols of the domain to express a new idea (Csikszentmihalyi, 1996). While it is unlikely that design students will change the nature of a discipline or culture through classroom projects, the challenge for faculty is to frame expectations in terms that will help them make such contributions in the future. Faculty substitute for "the field" in Csikszentmihalyi's model and inform their judgments by monitoring standards in the profession.

Csikszentmihalyi inventories the mental steps in the creative process: preparation in a set of issues that arises from curiosity, personal experience, or presented or discovered problems; incubation during which ideas percolate beneath the surface of consciousness; insight in which a good idea rises to the surface because it fits the problem well; evaluation in which the thinker decides if the idea is worth pursuing; and elaboration through which the thinker communicates the idea to others (Csikszentmihalyi, 1996). His argument that creative thinking involves more than inspiration, or the novel qualities of an artifact, suggests that faculty can structure class assignments in ways that reveal these various thinking behaviors. For example, engaging students in framing a problem tells faculty something about their curiosity and ability to synthesize experience and research through statements that focus creative behavior. Asking for justifications of choices among ideas—rather than telling students which ideas to pursue—provides insight into their judgment. The "product" of a classroom experience, in this sense, is the thinker, not the object.

Psychologist Robert Sternberg agrees that novelty alone is insufficient in assessing creative ideas. He holds that the appropriateness of solutions and the ability of the thinker to adapt to task constraints are essential (Sternberg

& Lubart, 1999). Concurring with Csikszentmihalyi, Sternberg suggests that creativity can be found in the synthetic ability to see problems in new ways, the analytical ability to recognize which ideas are worth pursuing, and the practical-contextual ability to persuade others of the value in new ideas (Sternberg & Lubart, 1999). At the same time, he cautions that too much of one ability and not enough of the others often results in ideas that have not undergone rigorous evaluation, ideas that are critically analytical but not creative, or poor ideas that are accepted simply because they are sold well (Sternberg & Lubart, 1999). Sternberg's advice argues for a finely detailed assessment of learning outcomes that separates analysis, synthesis, and presentation in the evaluation of student performance.

Recently promoted by IDEO founder David Kelley and former *Business Week* columnist Bruce Nussbaum, "design thinking" and its corollary "design innovation" attempt to distinguish a process-oriented response to design problems from broader notions of creativity. These concepts spawned a plethora of books by designers and business leaders that acknowledge value in observing stakeholders, brainstorming among experts from different fields, and rapid prototyping and testing of solutions that recognize value in failure.

In fact, "design thinking" originated under studies by British researchers Bruce Archer, Bryan Lawson, and Nigel Cross and as the title of a 1987 book by Peter Rowe. Cross described designers as: resolving ill-defined problems; adopting solution-focused cognitive strategies; employing the logic of conjecture; and using nonverbal modeling media in the solution of problems (Cross, 2006, p. 38). In contrast to the popular conception of the design process as a sequence of discrete steps that defer imagining solutions before completing research and the analysis of a problem, Cross's work showed that designers leap forward to an idea very quickly and then cycle back through more deliberate behaviors to confirm or refute initial perceptions (Cross, 2006).

Rosenman and Gero acknowledge the creative leap taken by many designers and identify the specific behaviors through which such insight might occur. They describe *combination* (bringing together ideas from existing sources), *mutation* (altering the features of something), *analogy* (using metaphor to generate a concept), *first principles* (identifying concepts at the heart of a problem), and *emergence* (finding new properties or affordances residing within an existing design) as specific creative behaviors through which new ideas spring to mind (Rosenman & Gero, 1993). This view is in opposition to students' popular beliefs that good ideas arrive on lightning bolts from the sky and cannot be prompted by intentional thinking strategies or perspectives on a problem. For faculty, it is possible to develop and assess students' thinking through activities structured to foreground these specific behaviors.

It is difficult to live up to ambitious definitions of creativity without also being critical. Philosopher John Dewey defined critical thinking as "[a]ctive, persistent, and careful consideration of a belief or supposed form of knowledge in light of the grounds that support it, and the future conclusions to which it attends" (Dewey, 1910, p. 6). In 1990, the *Delphi Report* of the American Philosophical Association expanded this definition by describing critical thinking as, "purposeful, self-regulatory judgment which results in interpretation, analysis, evaluation, and inference, as well as the evidential, conceptual, methodological, criteriological, or contextual considerations upon which judgment is based" (Facione, 2010, p. 23). Psychologist Diane Halpern characterizes critical thinking as directed to a desired outcome—as demonstrating a "willingness to plan, consider new options, try things in a new way, reconsider old problems, persist, and self-correct" (Halpern, 1998, p. 9).

Therefore, learning outcomes that address students' critical thinking across activities in design include the ability to: raise essential questions about the problem and frame them clearly and coherently; separate relevant from irrelevant information in the analysis of the problem; reach well-reasoned conclusions; test ideas against the constraints of the problem; and consider alternative points of view. Rarely do design faculty assess these critical behaviors as distinct skills or attribute the success or failure of students' design solutions to their application. More typically students receive evaluations of a general notion of "process," yet these individual competencies are easily addressed through instruction and provide students with greater detail regarding the assessment of their critical strengths and weaknesses.

Research also tells us something about students' attitudes toward critical and creative thinking as they enter college. Most first-year students are secure regarding their critical and creative-thinking skills (King & Kitchener, 1994), but alumni often indicate a drop in confidence when they confront the realities of the workplace. Recent graduates of design programs frequently complain that work assignments aren't as "interesting" as their class projects in school. What they are really saying is that they struggle to identify the creative challenge in work with more competing constraints than those defined by faculty—that professional projects don't arrive "interesting" but must be made so by the creative insight of the designer. These observations argue for greater investment by students in identifying and framing problems, as well as a larger role in selecting perspectives that guide problem-solving. If faculty artificially narrow problems, students cannot assess these skills.

Therefore, there is much to assess in thinking like a designer that is distinct from the products of such thought. And there are discrete thinking behaviors that go beyond simple definitions of "inspiration" or "process."

WHAT IS A RUBRIC?

A rubric is an evaluation tool that describes the criteria for student performance with respect to learning outcomes (Figure 5.1). Consistent with the desired outcomes assigned to a course or project, a rubric informs students of the level of expectations before work begins.

A *holistic rubric* reflects a general evaluation of student performance under a single grade. This approach gives students some idea of where they stand with respect to the overall expectations of a course or assignment, but it doesn't itemize particular strengths or weaknesses. As such, it tends to fall short in directing the student's attention to specific areas for improvement without further elaboration in conversation with faculty. In addition, holistic rubrics

FIGURE 5.1 *Rubrics.*

Outcome: Students will explain their methods and observations of user behavior and interpret their research findings in support of design decisions.

Rubrics for evaluating student achievement illustrate a continuum of performance with respect to the outcome:

Advanced – Written and visual explanations of methods and observations are coherent and tell a compelling, unified, and relevant story. Interpretations of research findings are insightful, original, and informative in framing design problems and guiding the direction of design activity.

Proficient – Written and visual explanations of methods and observations are coherent and complete. Interpretations of research findings are logical, defensible, and relevant to the design problem.

Developing – Written and visual explanations of methods and observations are accurate but incomplete and less than coherent in the use of language. Interpretations of research findings do not appear to be supported by evidence or guided by perceptions of an existing or potential design problem.

don't reveal to students any faculty weighting among different criteria or what distinguishes one grade from another.

An *analytical rubric* describes a student's product or performance through distinct characteristics and evaluates each one separately. It specifies the criteria used in making judgments and separates performances at various levels. Criteria may be weighted differently in arriving at an overall grade. Analytical rubrics provide more detail than holistic rubrics, thus explaining complex behaviors or various constraints to be satisfied by students' responses to assignments.

Imagine, for example, that an assignment asks students to analyze a design problem through research. The rubric for such an assignment might be described as *developing* if an analysis is limited to superficial descriptions and overgeneralizations with no supporting evidence. A more *proficient* account might include an overarching theory about the relationships among aspects of the problem but fragmentary evidence collected through a somewhat random application of research methods. By contrast, an *advanced* analysis not only is theoretically elegant and fully supported by examples but also shows systematic application of methods in collecting information and a personal point of view in its interpretation.

Using the same scale for evaluating students' creative thinking, *developing* creativity might be described as derivative or heavily dependent on faculty direction and satisfying only a few problem constraints in predictable ways. A more *proficient* approach might resolve a number of competing constraints through limited faculty coaching but not reflect a conscious choice among multiple perspectives on the problem. An *advanced* solution might reflect independent work that identifies a unique design challenge or perspective while also satisfying published criteria.

The use of a rubric makes the criteria for assessment public. Students have clear expectations of what is meaningful to success. Consistency in the application of standards across various students' performance explains why some students receive higher grades than others and sets a well-defined bar for improvement. When faculty frame rubrics in terms of observable behaviors, rather than by the qualities of artifacts alone, students know where to focus their efforts as they move forward.

There should be a direct relationship between the articulation of learning outcomes and the rubric for the evaluation of student performance as expressed in the syllabus or project brief, faculty's introduction of the assignment in class, critique comments, and the criteria applied in grading. Further, faculty should be prepared to use a full range of levels in describing student performance or the analytical rubric is: 1) not sufficiently ambitious (that is, all students achieve at the highest level in the rubric); 2) overly ambitious (that is, no exceptional students achieve at the higher levels of the rubric); or 3) vague in its description of what defines one level of student performance from another. For this reason, it is helpful to pilot rubrics over several semesters or projects.

The use of rubrics also reveals patterns in what students do or do not achieve as a group. These patterns tell faculty where to focus teaching efforts in subsequent assignments and identify content that may not be level appropriate. In doing so, the use of rubrics allows for mid-course redirection of teaching in specific ways that are likely to increase student success. Similarly, the use of rubrics can reveal recurring characteristics in an individual student's performance over time. This makes it possible for faculty to assess improvement.

CRITIQUES AND PEER-TO-PEER EVALUATION OF STUDENT WORK

It is equally important to be specific in class critiques and to develop in students the ability to make detailed evaluation of peer work. The critique is a time-honored tradition in design education—a feature of the signature pedagogy more recently discovered by others in the academy. Education professor Richard Light describes outcomes of the Harvard Assessment Seminars, in which undergraduate writing improved most when students met regularly with faculty and a small study group to critique each other's work (Light, 1990). Further, students considered classes in which peer review of their work was part of the course as the "most effective, most important courses" they had taken at Harvard (Light, 1990, p. 3. 5). When students knew peers would be reading their work, they approached it with greater seriousness because they didn't want to be embarrassed.

Education professor Jack Noonan studied all evaluation methods used across disciplines at Virginia Commonwealth University, including objective tests with right or wrong answers, written essays, oral presentations, and design critiques. He found the design critique the most successful at redirecting student behavior following failure. Under other forms of evaluation, students could identify content they hadn't mastered but did not know how to improve work habits for the next evaluation. Design students, on the other hand, could identify the consequences of specific decisions or ways of think-ing and had plans for improvement gained through critique comments.

Noonan's findings may also reflect how design is taught. In science, for example, students learn basic principles and then advance to application in subsequent courses without further evaluation of the specific content of earlier studies. If they fail to grasp rudimentary ideas or skills, they repeat content before moving on. Many engineering students, for example, take no engineering courses until they successfully complete a year of study in mathematics and basic sciences. Design education, however, places students in holistic problem-solving early in their curricular experiences. Design stu-dents typically learn basic principles and skills within a context for judging how and under what conditions they are useful. If they fail to understand a concept, principle, or skill, they can be sure it will appear again in future assignments, even when the focus of each project is very different. In other words, design students don't repeat assignments until they achieve mas-tery but, instead, demonstrate greater competency in constantly changing contexts.

Under the signature pedagogy of design critiques, all work is hung on the wall and discussed one project at a time by the class and the teacher or an invited jury. The presumption is that students learn from criticism of classmate's work; however, many students disengage until discussion of their own work occurs. Desk critiques involve faculty speaking one-on-one with individual students but rarely last more than ten or fifteen minutes, while the other students in the class typically do things that don't require interaction with faculty or peers.

It is time for faculty to be critical about critiques, to evaluate the effec-tiveness of evaluation formats through which students receive feedback about their work. There are a number of strategies for interim and final critiques that encourage active student participation in the critique process.

Small Group Critiques

Under this format, students critique work in groups of three to five students. If used for interim project feedback, students talk about their own work in groups determined randomly or by shared topical interests, methods used, or levels of achievement. Changing the composition of groups over the course of the project avoids group fatigue and diversifies points of view.

In using small groups for final critiques, students discuss three to five works other than their own and appoint a recorder to summarize comments for later presentation to the class. Under this strategy, students talk about work in greater depth and are more critical than in the public settings of full-class critiques. Reporting doesn't attribute specific comments to individuals but also includes minority opinions when there is disagreement. This practice of reporting group rather than individual perceptions increases the likelihood that students will be honest in their comments. Faculty are free to eavesdrop on conversations, thus evaluating students' performance as critics.

One Student/One Work Critiques

Under this approach, each student in the class critiques a single work of their choosing, but once the work has been discussed, it is eliminated from the inventory of possible choices. Students who haven't spoken maintain attention, mentally constructing a critique of future work with no assurance that the work they choose will remain in play as faculty move randomly through the class roll of critics. As the number of possible works gets smaller, critiques become more targeted. Faculty occasionally cycle back to previous speakers, asking questions about the relationship of current work to something from an earlier discussion. This format guarantees that all students speak at least once and that criticism doesn't depend solely on faculty.

Learning from the Elders

Students respect the opinions of their more advanced peers. Inviting upper-level students to critique the work of beginners demonstrates the insight gained through curricular experiences and is often more powerful than hearing the same criticism from faculty. In some cases, older students may have tackled the same assignment in their beginning years and make comments on the role of the assignment in their education as well as individual solutions.

Learning from Stakeholders

Many projects address particular audiences or users and acknowledge the relevance of experts from other professions (for example, engineers, builders, technologists, business strategists, marketers, etc.). Building a jury of people not directly related to design brings important insights to the critique process. In a critique of information designed for preschool children, for example, communication design students were confident they had nailed the characteristics of the audience in their solutions. They were embarrassed when the young children complained that the work for the critique was hung so high above their heads that they couldn't see it. It was an important lesson for designers that the process doesn't end with the prototype.

It is crucial to prepare visitors regarding the intent and structure of the critique process and to make sense of their comments with students after visitors leave the classroom. Typical users are unfamiliar with critiques and may be shy about making comments. Experts in other fields often provide criticism without linking it to important aspects of the contexts they represent. In some cases, comments by outsiders constitute a critique of the project rather than a critique of student work. Such criticism is informative to the faculty in framing future projects but not particularly useful to students in addressing the quality of their work. It is helpful to share with visitors the project constraints and learning outcomes students addressed and to discuss the scale or type of feedback that is beneficial to students in improving their performance.

Faculty also need to pay close attention to visitors' comments and discuss implications with students after visitors leave the critique. This means resisting the temptation to step in as an "interpreter" during criticism, which often undermines the credibility of the visitor or students' skill in reading audiences. At the same time, visitors' comments come from particular positions within the problem context and students need to be reminded of the value in understanding such positions: the technologist who knows deeply how systems work; the director of a woman's shelter who has firsthand experience of the need for security; or the contractor who must make sense of architects' plans.

Written Critiques

Sometimes students benefit from critiquing work without group discussion, from moments of quiet reflection. Written critiques of peer work require the construction of a critical argument that tells a classmate what is and isn't successful and why. On occasion, a single well-written critique may achieve more than talking about sixteen solutions to the same problem.

A variation on this process asks student designers to rank problem constraints in a written list next to their own work. Not only are the attributes of the solution open to critique but so is the designer's weighting of assignment variables. If the student values economy of form over meeting user needs, for example, then that is a topic for evaluation as well as a filter for consideration of the object.

Technologically Assisted Critiques

Survey software can deliver a faculty-authored rubric to each student's laptop during a student presentation. Students evaluate each project in real time, forwarding the results to the presenting student, who receives all feedback by the time he or she returns to a seat in the class. While there is little time to expand discussion beyond response to a very descriptive set of options, evaluations are informative regarding the outcomes the project was designed to achieve and the student's presentation abilities.

Outcome Critiques

Students often present work for critique through overly long rationales that account for every decision made along the way, relevant or not to the final solution and audience understanding of the problem. An alternative is to assign students to small groups and ask them to design a five-minute slide presentation of five things they learned by doing the project, using their work as visual examples of relevant concepts, principles, and skills. Such critiques often reveal accomplishments not evident in artifacts.

A variation on this approach is to focus presentation on the five most important aspects of the problem, also using their collective work to illustrate how design can address each aspect. This critique strategy not only focuses student attention on the purposes of the project rather than its history, but it also forces them to edit presentations by assessing and negotiating the strengths and weaknesses of individual solutions only with respect to stated outcomes. It prepares students for client presentations in which only observations essential to an argument make the cut.

A FEW WORDS ON DESIGN JURIES

Design juries are composed of outside professionals and originated at the École des Beaux-Arts in the seventeenth century. Experts reviewed student work, sometimes in closed rooms and at other times with students present. The practice is still a critical component of architecture pedagogy and occasionally can be found in the final reviews of other design fields. Researchers, including University of Illinois professor Kathryn H. Anthony in her book *Design Juries on Trial*, have studied the advantages and disadvantages of juries. Anthony's work found a number of recurring issues with respect to this review tradition.

First, students, faculty, and reviewers appear to have different opinions regarding the purpose of design juries. Students tend to view juries as evaluative, citing strengths and weaknesses in their solutions to particular problems. Faculty see them as opportunities to provide expert feedback to students that improves overall work. Practitioners describe them as practice for students in "selling their work" (Anthony, 1991). Anthony identifies a fundamental flaw of the jury system as goals of the review not being explicit, which often results in confusion (Anthony, 1991).

Students describe the best juries as having balance between positive and negative comments and as engaging students in the conversation. Students also appreciate reviewers from allied disciplines who bring new perspectives to the discussion of their work. The worst juries seem to involve heavy-handed, negative criticism, delivered in "overwhelmingly large doses" or an insensitive manner (Anthony, 1991, p. 33). The devastating effects of such critiques intensify when peers and important authority figures are present. Few other fields deliver feedback and evaluation to students in public settings. Students receive comments on written papers and grades on exams with no obligation to share their performance with others.

Generally, architecture students appear to favor interim juries rather than final juries (Anthony, 1991). Progress critiques allow them to make changes in work before final presentations and occur at times of less stress than final reviews. Anthony's research also found the characteristics of design students' lives increased stress. They spend more time in tighter spaces with the same peers than any other college students. Cloistered in the studio, they have few nondesign friends, poor diets, and irregular sleeping habits, averaging fewer than five hours of rest a night. Faculty often dismiss student complaints of unreasonable deadlines as routine indoctrination to the field that they survived in their own education. Through faculty attitudes toward these conditions and comments in juries, students perceive a "hidden curriculum" that communicates values and desired ways of behaving that have little to do with the actual content of courses (Anthony, 1991; Jackson, 1983).

MID-PROGRAM REVIEWS FOR ADVANCEMENT

Burgeoning interest in design study over the last two decades, particularly in communication and industrial design, has caused enrollment management problems for colleges and universities. Patterns of student interest don't always match the historic allocation of resources. For example, in a number of art departments, there is an inverse relationship between the distribution of tenured faculty across art and design majors and student interest in particular disciplines. It is often the case that faculty-to-student ratios are much higher in design than in fine arts and that departments solve the design faculty deficit through temporary part-time hires when funding is available. At the same time, institutions typically base department budgets on FTEs (full-time equivalent students), making them reluctant to turn away students from programs in high demand. In other words, design programs are often "cash cows," maintaining less popular majors in the department or college through overenrollment.

While enrollment problems could be resolved by admitting students in numbers directly proportional to fixed resources in various majors, many institutions accept students into a common first-year program and use a later review to screen for advancement into majors. This practice "kicks the can further down the road," deferring an inevitable decision until after students have spent a year or more in time and tuition pursuing a first-choice career they will never attain. In addition, the practice devotes disproportionate numbers of faculty to teaching students who may not even complete a degree in art or design.

In other schools, the mid-program review is used to eliminate low-performing students from advancing to upper-level study. The justification is that faculty require a common first year of study for students to demonstrate competencies. Others argue that eighteen-year-olds don't know what they want to study and that deferring the choice of a major encourages them to reflect on their interests and aptitudes.

This common evaluative practice has several disturbing consequences. First, the specific criteria for advancement are rarely published when students apply to schools. Students choose institutions with full expectation of completing the major of their choice. In reality, advancement from the freshman year often relies on evaluations of foundation portfolios, with no indication that faculty have agreed on explicit criteria. Students are often poor editors of their work, not knowing which examples best illustrate the undisclosed skills and insights faculty seek. As a result, faculty evaluations appear very subjective to students, particularly to those who are not successful in the review process.

Second, evaluation of foundation portfolios often bears little relationship to the grades students receive in courses that produced the work. In some cases, students receive As and Bs for first-year studio work but are denied admission to a major. It is also likely that some students with lower grades will be admitted. Problems, therefore, arise from grade inflation and a dual evaluation system. Former Duke University professor Stuart Rojstaczer compiles and describes grade inflation patterns in four-year programs in US colleges and universities over the last fifty years. Prior to 1963, before poor grades sent thousands of college-age men to Vietnam, the most popular grade used by faculty in assessing student performance was the "C." By 1998, faculty nationwide awarded "A" grades to roughly 45 percent of students in their classes. Grade inflation has continued to accelerate in an era of student consumerism that equates the right to high grades with the cost of a college education (Rojstaczer, 2016). Accurate or not, students view advancement reviews as a shadow evaluation system with criteria different from the ones applied to grading in the classroom—one that ultimately determines achievement of life goals.

In other cases, student review portfolios reflect the faculty who taught the course. When first-year courses are staffed by faculty from various majors, work under faculty in the major the student hopes to enter is often evaluated as more successful than work under faculty from another department—"It just looks more like the work we do" is the prevailing justification for admission to the major. Similar disparities occur when full-time faculty teach some sections of first-year coursework and inexperienced graduate teaching assistants or part-time faculty teach others. Under this system, students perceive advancement as the luck of the draw in their assignment to particular sections of first-year study.

Finally, institutions often provide little advising support for students who are rejected from their first-choice major. Less popular programs become the refuge for students who are perceived to be the least qualified. In other instances, students apply for transfer to another institution late in the admissions cycle or park themselves in majors they have no intention of completing, waiting for a second chance to apply to their first-choice major and extending their enrollment by another year with no guarantee of admission. Unsuccessful students may not receive counseling that would improve their chances at another school or in a second review. These situations mean that students often pay the penalty for program failure to assess student aptitude early in the admissions process and to manage enrollments within institutional resources. And all of these factors influence the retention and graduation rates institutions value in their assessment of programs.

On the other hand, there are programs that clearly articulate admissions criteria and set quotas for the number of students in specific majors when making decisions about the admission of students to the first-year program. Many of these programs maintain a common foundation curriculum for all majors and consider changes in majors after the first year, based on available spaces. Others divert some resources to teaching nonmajors who may discover the field through their initial design study but who also understand that a second-level admissions process will be necessary to continue in the field. While admissions criteria under these procedures clearly favor some indicators of success over others—for example, grade point average or drawing skills—students apply knowing priorities in institutional decisions, rather than learning of them one or two years later. The result is a presumption of success for all students, rather than certainty that some students will not achieve their educational goals.

Other programs use mid-program reviews as an advising strategy, rather than a threshold for admission to a major. Through these reviews faculty guide students in the choice of majors that match their interests and aptitudes, selection of electives, and development of professional plans. Mid-program reviews are also a good time for faculty to assess the progress of a student cohort and to adjust curricular options based on findings. In these cases, review outcomes are not punitive.

EVALUATING CURRICULAR EFFECTIVENESS

Curricular assessment is longitudinal; it requires observation and collection of findings over time, not in the months before a major review. Most colleges and universities require periodic reviews of curricula, with some also conducting external reviews through accrediting agencies or teams of experts convened by the institution. The purpose of these reviews is to engage programs in continuous improvement and to provide administrators with evidence of effective operations and curricular success. The content, format, and timing of such reviews are typically determined at the level of the chief academic officer of the institution and favor metrics that can be compared across the institution. It is also important for programs to evaluate curricular issues that are specific to the discipline and of interest to the faculty.

In general, comprehensive program reviews examine two types of issues: operational and instructional. Operational issues include concerns such as:

- Articulation of mission, goals, and objectives
- Size and scope of curricula in relation to resources
- Enrollment and resource allocation
- Facilities
- Governance and decision-making structures
- Faculty numbers, qualifications, and professional development
- Recruitment, advising, and recordkeeping
- Student retention and graduation rates
- Evaluation and planning activities

Instructional concerns include the quality and productivity of programs with respect to mission, goals, and objectives, as well as the success of students upon graduation. Reviewers look for positive relationships among projection, planning, and evaluation as described in chapter 2 of this book. Most reviews by accreditors or external reviewers require a self-study written by faculty in the program. Reviewers expect the self-study to be evaluative, citing strengths and weaknesses with respect to published mission, goals, and objectives, not simply descriptive. Too often self-studies include lengthy narratives of fact without any evaluative analysis that informs projection and planning.

Art and design faculty typically engage in a variety of assessment activities but are notoriously remiss in documenting the outcomes and use of results. Faculty tinker with courses based on individual impressions of success, and in a few years nothing about the curriculum resembles the original plan. Faculty come and go, making it impossible to reconstruct how things came to be the way they are. And when administrators and accrediting agencies ask for rationales to support current practices, there is little record of actions taken to change the course of study since the last review. It is critical to generate and archive a consistent set of assessment documents, such as minutes of curriculum retreats, curriculum approval forms, and any evaluative summaries completed by faculty and administration. Every end-of-year portfolio review is evidence of curriculum assessment as well as evaluation of individual student performance. It is a simple matter to ask faculty to summarize the results of a review as consistent or inconsistent with each of the published student learning outcomes. Areas that come up short can form the agenda for periodic curriculum discussions.

Programs need to decide how often to evaluate student achievement of particular competencies. For example, if there is a general perception that design history is not informing student work in studios, then evaluating the use of precedence may be more urgent than other outcomes. Likewise, if an outcome targets improving students' writing skills, reaching conclusions on the basis of freshmen work may be premature. It is important not to exhaust faculty by evaluating everything all the time. Any assessment plan should be sustainable and meaningful.

SUMMARY

Faculty must remember that the "unit of measurement" in evaluative activities is the student—the development of knowledge, skills, attitudes, and values gained through curricular experiences. Products provide insight into students' critical and creative thinking, but the goal of instruction is to develop the competencies described in student-centered learning outcomes for later transfer to novel problems. Rubrics publicly articulate a graded structure of knowledge and skills that distinguish various levels of student performance. Analytical rubrics itemize aspects of performance as a means for guiding student improvement. While the critique process is a component of the signature pedagogy of design, faculty must evaluate the continuing effectiveness of traditional critique strategies. Curricular assessment should be ongoing and include documentation of findings and the use of results. Institutions value comprehensive curricular assessments that include a detailed self-study process as well as external evaluation.

PART II
TEACHING *THROUGH* DESIGN

D esign-based teaching and learning borrows the methods of design practice and the pedagogy of design education in teaching a variety of subjects and thinking skills in both K–12 schools and higher education. The intent of this work is not to produce professional designers or even to inform future clients for design practice but to encourage critical and creative thinking in any discipline through the signature pedagogy of design. The subject of thought, in this case, is far less important than the type of thinking in which students engage.

In 1992, the US Department of Labor sought to reinforce new demands on education asserted by work in the twenty-first century. In defining essential competencies and thinking skills, the Secretary's Commission on Achieving Necessary Skills (SCANS) report called for creative thinking and problem-solving, seeing things in the mind's eye, reasoning, and knowing how to learn rather than mastering specific facts and technical skills as characteristic of today's productive adults.

Yet despite this and other calls for educational reform, standardized testing continues to encourage drill-and-kill, rote memorization approaches to learning in K–12 schools—recall of facts over higher-order thinking. Further, reform efforts articulate goals and subject area content but remain relatively silent on pedagogical strategies. The preservice and in-service education of teachers often focuses on curricular mandates but leaves teachers unprepared to do little more than deliver scripted material from an approved textbook or curriculum plan. In other words, colleges and universities often fail to view teachers as designers of learning experiences.

The SCANS report described learning outcomes that are consistent with those of a college design education; the attributes of people who earn a four-year degree under pedagogies developed over the last century specifically to produce such thinking skills. And although application of design-based content and pedagogy has a long history in primary and secondary education, interest at the college level is more recent and driven by changes in the nature of work and the need for innovation in all areas of scholarship.

The transformation of work in the twenty-first century recommends this approach to education. Roger Martin at the University of Toronto described a dramatic shift from routine-oriented service work, in which people do the same thing each day, to creative work, in which efforts are directed toward producing something new.

Economist Richard Florida disputes the central thesis of Thomas Friedman's book *The World Is Flat*, which suggests that there is a level playing field in the global economy brought about by computing and the dominance of multinational companies. Instead, Florida argues in a 2005 *Atlantic Monthly* article that "The World Is Spiky," with hills and valleys of economic opportunity. The hills are centers of innovation, supported globally by centers of manufacturing with slightly less opportunity (Florida, 2005). Florida's valleys are places where there is little hope of ever competing economically. Creative thinking, therefore, is at the center of Florida's thesis in establishing clustered centers of innovation.

The following chapters address the history of design in K-12 schools and offer specific examples of pedagogical strategies that encourage critical and creative thinking. While they focus on addressing standards for which today's K-12 teachers are accountable, they scale easily to college-level teaching and learning.

CHAPTER 6:
DESIGN IN THE SERVICE OF TEACHING

DESIGN THINKING

Ask any two designers to define *design* and you're likely to get very different answers. For some it is a noun that describes the expressive and functional attributes of artifacts and environments crafted through professional expertise. For others, it is a verb that refers to problem-solving activities such as planning and prototyping. And for others it is a discipline or domain with its own ways of knowing and doing.

For much of modern history, people relied on designers to make things look and work better, to solve problems of limited scope using craft-based know-how acquired through professional education and practice. Today's leaders, however, search for innovation strategies that respond to complex environmental, social, technological, and economic problems—challenges that resist solution through linear, hierarchical processes of the past. Their concerns are not only for greater access to professionals who specialize in creative work but also for a larger innovation workforce that responds to the knowledge economy in ways very different from the industrial age. Others seek ways to humanize a world increasingly shaped by technology—to expand human potential with the fewest negative consequences for today's fragile environmental, social, and economic systems. These expectations make demands on education to develop critical and creative thinkers in all fields who prepare for a world of ambiguous problems, rapid change, and expanding complexity.

Interest in design thinking has a long history. Nobel Prize laureate Herbert Simon wrote in his 1969 *The Sciences of the Artificial*, "[e]veryone designs who devises courses of action aimed at changing existing situations into preferred ones" (Simon, 1969, 1996, p. 111). He argued that the natural sciences are concerned with how things are, while design is uniquely concerned with how things ought to be. Philosopher and urban planner Donald Schön counterbalanced Simon's description of a "science of design" by saying that designers deal with messy, problematic situations that demand intuitive and reflective practices—that the nature of design problems is uncertainty and conflicting values in contrast to the well-formed questions of science (Schön, 1983).

Stanford University engineering professor Robert McKim taught courses and wrote on the importance of developing visual thinking as a complement to computational and linguistic forms of thought. His 1972 *Experiences in Visual Thinking* described visual and spatial reasoning as essential skills not developed by schools but important in a world that depends increasingly on visual information. Harvard design professor Peter Rowe titled his 1987 book, *Design Thinking*, to reveal the structure and focus of inquiry during private moments of invention. And IDEO and Stanford d. school founder David Kelley and his colleagues adapted the design process for broader application in business and innovative problem-solving that goes beyond the creation of artifacts.

Claims that design represents a distinct way of knowing—a domain separate from science and the humanities—were supported by a 1979 British Department of Education and Science research project led by Bruce Archer at the Royal College of Art. Titled *Design in General Education*, the project recognized three distinct views of knowledge in social, cultural, and educational systems. The researchers acknowledged the dominance of science and the humanities or arts but also identified design as a third domain—as "the conception and realization of new things" arising from the application of "planning, inventing, making and doing" (Cross, 2006, p. 17). They attributed educational neglect in developing students' design competencies to the lack of articulation about its "things to know, ways of knowing them, and ways of finding out about them" (Cross, 2006, p. 17).

The report went on to compare the three knowledge domains with respect to the phenomenon of study, appropriate methods of inquiry, and belief systems and values of the culture (Figure 6.1: Cross 2006, pp. 17–18). Although today's design practices appear to blur the boundaries among these domains through interest in both the subjective qualities of users' experiences and the science of environmental and technological systems, authors of the

	Science:	Humanities/arts:	Design:
Phenomenon of study:	The natural world	Human experience	The artificial world
Appropriate methods:	Controlled experiment, classification, analysis	Analogy, metaphor, evaluation	Modeling, pattern-formation, synthesis
Values:	Objectivity, rationality, neutrality, and concern for "truth"	Subjectivity, imagination, commitment, and concern for "justice"	Practicality, ingenuity, empathy, and concern for "appropriateness"

FIGURE 6.1 *A study by the Royal College of Art under the British Department of Education and Science distinguished among three domains of knowledge: science, humanities, and design. The first two are addressed by traditional education, but design is less well understood as an essential area of human knowledge and activity (Cross, 2006, p. 18).*

report worried less about the specific subject matter of designers' work than the type of thinking necessary to accomplish it.

The researchers also described visual/spatial reasoning as characteristic of design. In this sense, modeling, diagramming, and sketching are ways of thinking, not simply methods of communication. They convert hazy impressions to concrete form and allow designers to manipulate concepts in the physical world. Psychologist Jerome Bruner believes people use different modes of thinking continuously, rather than pass through them sequentially in developmental stages as suggested by Jean Piaget (Cross, 2006, p. 28). This view of thinking means that education can develop students' literacy, numeracy, and visual/spatial reasoning from lower to higher levels and teach students to move flexibly from one to the next as appropriate to the task. Curricula in K-12 schools and colleges, however, tend to organize learning experiences under sequential interpretations of Piaget's model, decreasing engagement in concrete "making" activities as students progress in age and level of study. Advanced students often become readers, not makers of visual form, failing to develop visual/spatial reasoning as part of their problem-solving repertoire.

Changes in the nature of contemporary life and work generate broad interest in the particular characteristics of design as a domain. Studies of education call for new competencies that are remarkably similar to the thinking behaviors of designers, suggesting that the pedagogy of design education may hold relevance for expanding problem-solving strategies in other fields.

THE ROLE OF DESIGN THINKING IN EDUCATION

In 1992, the US Department of Labor published the Secretary's Commission on Achieving Necessary Skills (SCANS) report. It outlined competencies required by work in the twenty-first century and, by implication, the outcomes expected from education (Figure 6.2). A number of issues in this report acknowledged the shift from an industrial economy to a knowledge-based one.

The inclusion of *creative thinking*, *decision-making*, and *problem-solving* as discrete thinking skills is a sign to educators that each requires specific attention in curriculum and instruction. While the literature on these behaviors is deep, there is little evidence that it informs the preservice education of K-12 teachers or general instruction for college students across fields. In institutional research for a campus-wide project to improve student learning at NC State University, for example, faculty cited developing critical and creative thinking as their top priority. At the same time, they admitted that most faculty don't know how to teach such skills and focus only on factual knowledge related to their discipline (NC State University, 2014).

Competencies for productive work	Foundation for mastery and use of competencies	
	Thinking skills	Personal qualities
Use of resources	Creative thinking	Responsibility
Use of information	Decision-making	Self-esteem
Interpersonal skills	Problem solving skills	Sociability
Using systems	Seeing things in the mind's eye	Self-management
Using technology	Knowing how to learn	Integrity
	Reasoning	

FIGURE 6.2 *In 1992, the US Department of Labor described the demands work in the twenty-first century places on education. These essential competencies reflect a knowledge economy very different from the industrial age that inspired many long-standing school curricula and pedagogical approaches.*

Seeing things in the mind's eye not only reinforces Robert McKim's advocacy for visual/spatial reasoning—that we can think in pictures as well as words and numbers—but also Herbert Simon's notion of imagining a preferred state of things. *Abductive reasoning* is the logic of conjecture, of suggesting theories of action based on observation. Abductive reasoning is not about proof. It is about inference—speculative and propositional explanations of why things are the way they are and how they might be different under some future action. Schools and colleges typically teach deductive reasoning (reaching conclusions by applying general rules to evidence) and inductive reasoning (developing rules from specific cases). They are less likely, however, to teach students to devise and weigh options in the face of ambiguous situations. Contemporary problems are poorly defined. Their boundaries are unclear, and their constraints are both unstable and interdependent, making it difficult to prove cause and effect. In many cases, waiting for proof is paralyzing. It is through abductive reasoning that designers propose theories of action that move things forward.

SCANS also identified the *use of resources, information, technology*, and *systems* as competencies for productive work. While the importance of the first three is obvious, the *use of systems* requires some explanation and acknowledges the scale at which contemporary problems exist. Under an industrial paradigm, work was at the level of components and products, and technology developed to meet specific needs. Industry tinkered with product attributes, one at a time, in efforts toward incremental improvement in meeting known needs. New products required repetition of full development and manufacturing cycles for each new item, and the stopping condition in such work was "almost perfect."

The problems of postindustrial society, on the other hand, exist at the scale of systems, and technology arrives before we fully understand what it is good for. It is no longer possible to ignore consequences far beyond the component or product. For instance, a cultural commitment to anytime/anywhere personal transportation through the automobile shapes the configuration of cities, use of natural resources and land, air quality, traffic congestion, safety, development of public transportation systems, and perceived social status of users. Today's technology evolves through iterations as society finds new uses never imagined in its initial development. The self-driving car was something unthinkable only decades ago and has enormous implications for culture. The Internet, for example, started as communication for scientists and the military, not as a strategy for commerce, education, or social interaction. Development of these systems requires research and collaboration across disciplines. The stopping condition for contemporary work under these conditions is "good enough for now" as the culture adapts and changes surrounding conditions. The methods for planning, developing, and managing complex systems cannot be the same as those of the industrial age.

The SCANS report also recognizes that it is not possible for students to acquire all knowledge in twelve years of primary and secondary education and that knowledge will change between graduation from college and the end of a professional career. The inclusion of *learning how to learn* anticipates exponential growth in knowledge and ongoing changes in the content and nature of work. It raises questions regarding the value of rote memorization and drill-and-kill pedagogical strategies. Instead, it emphasizes that students must adapt learning to the content and situations in which new knowledge is required.

Demands for critical and creative thinking have increased since the Department of Labor studies in the 1990s. Roger Martin of the Prosperity Institute at the University of Toronto made a compelling case that the future of high-wage work is in creative industries, not in routine service work that requires people to do the same thing every day. Martin described a decline in physical work, a statistical plateauing of routine service work, and an increase in creativity-oriented jobs that engage people in the critical analysis and judgment that it takes to make something new (Martin, 2009). In a 2009 study, Martin described 42 percent of the new jobs created in the preceding decade in the United States as being creativity oriented. He emphasized the importance of *analytical skills* (determining how systems work, comparing and contrasting patterns, using rules and methods to solve problems) and *social intelligence skills* (collaborating, negotiating, managing, deductive thinking), showing that earnings rise most for graduates who can apply general rules to specific problems and produce solutions that make sense (Martin, 2009, p. 12). Wages overall are dramatically higher for people in creativity-oriented occupations, and creative workers experience more stable employment in tough economic times than those in routine-oriented work (Martin, 2009).

A 2013 study (Figure 6.3) asked workers in innovation jobs to rank nineteen qualities necessary for success in their work. In almost all cases, four attributes at the top of people's lists were: 1) come with new ideas; 2) willing to question ideas; 3) present ideas to an audience; and 4) alert to opportunities

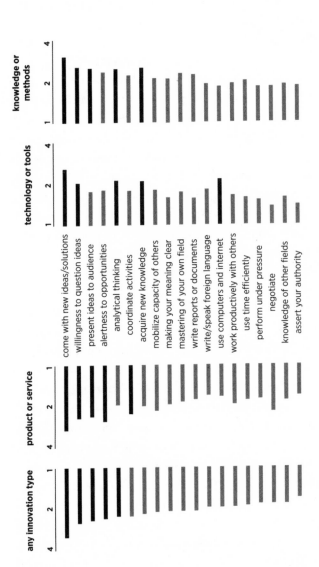

FIGURE 6.3 *From a study by Avvisati, Jacotin, and Vincent-Lancrin titled "Educating Higher Education Students for Innovative Economies: What International Data Tell Us." This 2013 study asked respondents to rate from 1 to 4 the importance of nineteen skills in their innovation jobs and their self-assessed skill levels in these competencies. Researches also asked respondents about the relationship between college faculty's various pedagogical approaches and their development of the nineteen skills.*

(Avvisati et al., 2013, p. 230). Respondents also ranked analytical thinking toward the top of their lists, but its importance varied for the type of industry. Mastery in one's own field ranked tenth overall. In other words, the study showed that innovation work valued critical and creative thinking over specific disciplinary knowledge.

The study asked the same college graduates to assess the top strengths and weaknesses of their education. Graduates worldwide tended to agree that colleges do a good job at teaching analytical skills and the ability to acquire new knowledge, as well as domain-specific expertise. However, students were generally dissatisfied with development of their social skills—collaboration, communication, and leadership (Avvistati et al., 2013). The study also asked graduates about pedagogies used in college classrooms, separating instruction in theory (represented by lectures and the teacher as the main source of information) from practice (represented by group assignments, research projects, project- or problem-based learning, internships, practical knowledge, and oral presentations by students). Although theory-based forms of instruction positively influenced graduates' work in innovation jobs, its effect was seen by graduates as significantly weaker than that of engagement in practice-based instruction (Avvistati et al., 2013). In addition, the higher the emphasis on theory-based instruction in their studies, the more students reported analytical skills as strong points in their education, and the higher the emphasis on practice-based instruction in their studies, the more students reported creative skills as strong points in their education (Avvistati et al., 2013).

A report by the Organization for Economic Cooperation and Development (OECD)—*The Innovation Imperative: Contributing to Productivity, Growth, and Well-Being*—reported that problem-based learning is increasingly used to foster innovation in a variety of fields. The studies cited in the report indicated that situated learning overcomes students' sense of overload with "isolated concepts that lack authentic context" (OECD, 2015, p. 55). They also reported that problem-based learning increases long-term knowledge retention and application, while also building social intelligence skills such as teamwork (OECD, 2015). However, problem-based learning is shown to be less effective in short-term retention, having some negative influence on immediate test scores (OECD, 2015). This last finding is cautionary for schools and colleges regarding the metrics for measuring outcomes of curricular change.

The pedagogy of a discipline, therefore, influences students' approaches to their work and worldviews that guide their problem-solving. In a 1972 study,

British psychologist and design researcher Bryan Lawson asked two groups of students in their final year of college—engineers and architects—to build flat structures using a set of differently colored blocks. They were given an incomplete set of rules for the structure and asked to determine the unknown rules governing a predetermined solution. The scientists tested all possible combinations of the blocks to see if they could determine the unknown rules from the variations. The architects proposed rules and then tested them one at a time, discarding rules as they went along until they arrived at the acceptable solution. In other words, the scientists were problem focused and analytical while the architects were solution focused and favored synthesis. Lawson then tested first-year students but found no differences in their strategies, concluding that the students' approaches were products of how they were taught in their respective disciplines.

These arguments for a critical and creative-thinking approach to contemporary problems and studies of how students learn suggest that the very outcomes sought by government and business may be found in the methods of design and the pedagogy of design education. In fact, graduates of college-level design programs exhibit the very competencies outlined in the SCANS report, and the pedagogy of design education closely resembles the strategies to which college graduates attribute their creative development. The task lies in articulating how design translates as a teaching and learning strategy in other disciplines.

THE LEGACY OF DESIGN IN K–12 SCHOOLS

The earliest American work in design-based education began as efforts by professional designers to explain to students the role design plays in the built world. Often focused on the design of products, buildings, and cities, these efforts piggybacked on increasing public concern for developing a citizenry capable of making informed decisions about the quality of life in communities (Davis et al., 1997).

In 1970, architects Richard Saul Wurman and Alan Levy formed the Group for Environmental Education (GEE). Through *Our Man-Made Environment: Book Seven*, GEE engaged Philadelphia middle school students in activities about the design of urban spaces and the built environment. The book explained why we build our environment and the forces that determine the form the environment takes. Wurman followed this work with a series of activity-oriented publications for primary-grade students titled *The Process of Choice*, which explained that products and environments result from values-oriented decision-making about what people want and need, as well as available resources. Wurman would later found the popular TED (Technology, Entertainment, Design) conferences, recognized internationally for short, powerful speeches with a related intent to reveal how the world's innovators think on a wide range of important topics.

In 1975, Cranbrook Academy of Art published *Problem Solving in the Man-made Environment*, a program for seventh-grade social studies students in five hundred Michigan public schools. The program encouraged intelligent analyses of communication, products, and environments and their social effects through a series of posters—books on walls—and sixty-five student projects described in a teacher's manual. With the goal of integrating design issues into the existing social studies curriculum, hands-on activities used the school and community to demonstrate how design shapes the social as well as the physical character of the environment. The program was funded by the Michigan Council for the Arts, which later supported Design Michigan, a similar program for adults in business and government.

Buildings and cities were an entry point for a number of curriculum developers. Ginny Graves's Center for Understanding the Built Environment, Doreen Nelson's Center for City Building Education, and Sharon Sutton's Urban Network involved school children and their teachers in community planning as a strategy for understanding how the built environment works at a variety of levels. Ann Taylor's School Zone Institute at the University of New Mexico focused on the relationship between school design and curriculum, using college-level architecture students in workshops and activities with K-12 students. Nelson taught at a Los Angeles elementary school across the street from designer Charles Eames's professional office. Eames supported her "backward thinking" approach to learning, which asks children to imagine what they want and need and then leads them through processes for making things happen. Nelson later established a master's program in teaching through design at California Polytechnic State University/Pomona. The program was distinguished by her active engagement with teachers in their school classrooms, rather than in university facilities.

Charles Burnette initiated a design-based K-12 program at the University of the Arts while director of the program in Industrial Design. The university's K-12 design work began as an extension of Burnette's course *Design with Kids*.

Funded through grants, the program trained teachers in a seven-step design process. Although it started as an enrichment program for practicing teachers, the approach later found a curricular home in the university's Art Education program. The International Technology Education Association (now the International Technology and Engineering Educators Association) centered its work on the application of design problem-solving to the invention of technology. It advocated the transformation of what was once called "industrial arts" in K-12 schools, often focusing on robotics and maker technologies. This work evolved as "engineering design" in a number of contemporary K-12 curricula.

In most cases, early programs were "proofs of concept" that design could be integrated with existing K-12 curricula and that young children could master problem-solving related to the built world. These initiatives depended on the active involvement of their authors and funding from outside school budgets. Many disappeared when their developers moved on to other things. Nelson's program at Cal Poly is as an exception, and through her extended affiliation with Art Center College of Design, summer workshops offer regular continuing education opportunities for teachers in her approach to teaching and learning.

While American designers were experimenting in schools, the British government's Schools Council and Department of Education and Science argued successfully for the inclusion of Design and Technology as a discrete subject area in the national curriculum. Prior to this effort, aspects of design education could be found in courses in home economics, woodworking, textiles, electronics, and other vocational areas of the curriculum. The Royal College of Art study on *Design in General Education* introduced writings by Bruce Archer, Nigel Cross, Ken Baynes, and Brian Lawson on issues of design thinking, which continue to be seminal references among many perspectives on the topic. Cross's *Designerly Ways of Knowing* and Lawson's *How Designers Think* predate the current plethora of books on design thinking, innovation, and creativity written to satisfy the appetite of business for new approaches to management and product/service development.

Some say the earliest Design and Technology curriculum in the United Kingdom was put together hastily and without adequate teacher training to support ambitious learning outcomes. The British Department of Education and Science called for evaluation of student performance in 1991. The British School Examination and Assessment Council (SEAC) charged Goldsmiths'

College professor Richard Kimbell, who headed the Technology Education Research Unit, with leading a national study of student achievement in design and technology.

The British assessment team defined design as "the purposeful pursuit of a task to some form of resolution that results in improvement (for someone) in the made world" (Kimbell et al., 1991, p. 17) and determined that the made world was comprised of "products, systems, and environments in which they function" (Kimbell et al., 1991, p. 18). The team showed less agreement about a definition of the design process, however. They rejected descriptions of design as a linear or cyclical sequence of task-oriented steps for what they saw as a somewhat messier, interactive process. The assessment team worried that describing steps would encourage "greater concern for 'doing' all the stages of the process, than for combining a growing range of capabilities in a way which reflects individual creativity and confident and effective working methods" (Kimbell et al., 1991, p. 19). Some K–12 design programs in the United States show this tendency, so British fears were well founded that a linear process could dominate more authentic thinking in design.

Agreeing that the fundamental issue in design was the ability to "convert active capabilities into passive products," Kimbell's team ultimately described a relationship between mind and hand in which a range of thinking behaviors (hazy impressions > speculation and exploration > clarification and validation > critical appraisal) produce tangible artifacts (discussions, drawings, diagrams and graphs, models, prototypes, or provisional solutions) (Kimbell et al., 1991, p. 20).

The study reached many conclusions, describing student performance systematically under an inventory of the procedural, communication, and conceptual qualities of design, which together produced a holistic score for each student (Davis & Littlejohn, 2016). The test was authentic to design in its performance-based activity and scored independently by multiple reviewers, whose evaluations were in strong agreement about student achievement (Kimbell et al., 1991). This national assessment demonstrated that what many view as the "subjective" evaluation of portfolios could produce statistically significant correlations among the scores of expert reviewers when they work within a well-defined framework of standards (Davis & Littlejohn, 2016).

Twenty-five years later, a National Curriculum Review would threaten instruction in Design and Technology in the United Kingdom. Studies questioned whether there was a suitable level of challenge for students in the subject area and whether curricular content adequately prepared students for more advanced academic and vocational education. A revised curriculum, which moved the subject from its crafts roots of the industrial age to high technology, is scheduled for implementation in 2017. The Department of Education announced that: "The content emphasises the iterative design processes that all students should understand and be able to demonstrate and which is at the core of contemporary practice. It will allow both breadth and depth of knowledge, without limiting students on the materials they can work with, enabling them to make choices appropriate to their design, rather than creating a design around a particular material" (Gibb, 2015).

Project-based or problem-based learning captured the attention of American schools as a teaching strategy in the 1990s. K-12 classroom teachers discovered that scenario-driven teaching and learning strategies held relevance for various school subjects. Design projects were consistent with this approach. The National Endowment for the Arts commissioned a two-year study of design in K-12 schools to ascertain the impact of previous NEA funding on the application of design in American classrooms. Through a hotline advertised in teacher journals, the study identified more than nine hundred K-12 teacher nominees who used some form of design-based pedagogy or included specific design content in their curricula. Unlike earlier efforts under designer's authorship and guidance, these were classroom teachers who adopted design-based practices without the assistance of professionals. *Design as a Catalyst for Learning* reached a number of conclusions about the positive impact of design approaches on teaching and learning. The report indicated that design activities:

- Enhanced students' flexibility in thinking skills;
- Strengthened approaches to creative problem-solving;
- Promoted self-directed learning;
- Applied classroom experiences to everyday life;
- Increased student comfort with uncertainty;
- Built relationships across school subjects;
- Developed communication skills and teamwork; and
- Cultivated responsible citizens (Davis et al., 1997).

However, the study also found that there was little systematic evaluation of these teaching practices or direct evidence of students' improved content

mastery in core subjects, other than through the anecdotal accounts of nom-
inated teachers (Davis et al., 1997). Further, most teachers reported that they
acquired their knowledge of design and design methods largely through
informal exposure to designers, not through preservice training (Davis et al.,
1997). Art teachers, in particular, were under-represented in the study, not in
the number of nominations but in the content of case studies that viewed
design as something more than the arrangement of abstract form. Of the 169
classroom applications selected for *Design as a Catalyst for Learning*, only two
were from art teachers. The study also found that design-based teachers typically worked alone in their pedagogical approach, without the active participation of colleagues or school administrators. These concerns raised questions
regarding how design-based practices could be scaled to the levels of schools
and districts, as well as how design content might enter the college curricula
of teacher preparation programs.

There were major differences, therefore, between early efforts in the
United States and United Kingdom regarding design in K–12 schools. In
the United States, design served as a general strategy for teaching and learning rather than as discrete subject matter in the curriculum. Design-based
approaches were adopted through self-initiated teacher interest rather than
the systematic curriculum change under government direction in the United
Kingdom (Davis & Littlejohn, 2016). In the United States, evaluation of
design-based pedagogies relied on anecdotal reporting by individual teachers
versus the rigorous national assessment of curricular outcomes and measurable
evidence of student achievement in British schools. There was no American
consensus regarding theories of action underpinning design-based instruction
and no uniform metrics for measuring student achievement, other than a
general sense of addressing the curricular mandates to which all teachers in a
district or state were accountable (Davis & Littlejohn, 2016). Perceptions of
the efficacy of a design approach to instruction in the United States depended
on individual interpretation and ranged from design as a distinct discipline
of study to its role as a delivery system for other content in the curriculum.

Concurrent with these studies of design education in the United States
and United Kingdom, the national movement to articulate content standards in core subject areas gained momentum in American schools. Congress enacted *Goals 2000* in 1994, an effort to raise academic standards in
the nation's classrooms through common definitions of what "every young
American should know and be able to do" in twelve academic subject areas.

Design concepts appeared in the voluntary content standards of several disciplines—most notably in science, civics, and language arts.

The American Association for the Advancement of Science, in *Benchmarks for Science Literacy*, made explicit references to design, stating that the goal of science literacy is in part, to help people "make sense of how the natural and designed worlds work" (AAAS, 1993, p. xi). The *National Science Education Standards* acknowledged that very young children could carry out design activities before they engaged in scientific inquiry and could analyze constraints through the design of communication, products, and environments. The national standards distinguished between science and technology, defining the latter as a response to human problems, needs, or aspirations. Studies by the National Research Council found that high school students "respond positively to the concrete, practical, outcome orientation of design before they are able to engage in the abstract, theoretical nature of many scientific inquiries" (National Research Council, 1996, p. 191). This interest in design continues in the more recent *Next Generation Science Standards* (released in 2013) and the work of the National Academy of Engineering in testing students' technology and design literacy (conducted in 2014).

The *National Standards for Civics and Government* encouraged students to conduct research in their communities, meet with stakeholders, and build coalitions (Center for Civic Education, 1994, p. 5), often dealing with issues related to the built environment and communication. *National Geography Standards* asked young students to study "the spatial organization of people, places, and environments . . . processes, patterns, and functions of human settlements . . . how humans modify the physical environment" (Geography Education Standards Project, 1994). By high school, geography students were "to analyze the structure and shapes of cities and to predict the environmental impact of changes in population, transportation, and economic activity" (Davis et al., 1997, p. 63).

Language Arts Standards published by the National Council of Teachers of English and the International Reading Association referred to mastery of visual as well as verbal language. They asked students to pose problems and solve them by analyzing and synthesizing information from "nonprint" texts. Presenting stories in nonprint media, including film and video, and extracting information from maps, charts, photographs, and other graphic material were central to the standards (Davis et al., 1997).

Despite this interest in design-related content among the core disciplines at both national and state levels, design was all but missing in the visual arts standards where one might expect even greater affinity. Instead of describing thinking skills characteristic of the discipline, the 1994 *National Visual Arts Standards* listed design as a medium with clay, wood, and stained glass. When challenged on this misrepresentation of the discipline as accountable to the thinking processes and self-defined constraints of painters and sculptors, authors of the standards offered ambiguous references to "function" and "structure" as justification of their attention to design (Consortium of National Art Education Associations, 1994). This position ran counter to the findings of the study by the Royal College of Art that design is a "third discipline," residing somewhere between the humanities and science with its own ways of knowing and things to know.

Much of this confusion about the relationship between art and design could be traced to trends in art education across the preceding decade. By the 1990s, the Getty Education Institute for the Arts had transformed the preservice education of art teachers and art curricula in many K–12 schools through its Discipline-Based Art Education (DBAE) approach to visual education. Under this widely promoted, well-funded framework, the study of art was divided into four disciplines: production, history, criticism, and aesthetics. Although the published intent of the initiative was to include design as relevant subject matter, no significant efforts were made on behalf of the discipline.

Penn State University art educator Brent Wilson authored a ten-year assessment of DBAE for the Getty titled *The Quiet Evolution*, in which he cited the absence of mature histories of design as the reason schools ignored the field (Wilson, 1997). This weak explanation overlooked a long lineage of historical scholarship in architecture and design and a number of important journals and research societies devoted almost exclusively to design history, as well as more recent chronologies of graphic and industrial design history that were well into second and third editions at the time of Wilson's evaluation. In addition, alternate histories—such as Stuart Ewen's *All-Consuming Images: The Politics of Style* and Penny Sparke's *Introduction to Design and Culture*—traced the evolution of design from outside the famous-people/famous-objects canon of art history, focusing instead on technological, social, and economic conditions that shaped design responses. It was during the Getty years that postmodern scholars and writers obsessed over rethinking historical perspectives and critical theories of design, so Wilson's assessment that there was limited discourse rang false. It was more believable that the absence of design in the Getty's work resulted from the absence of design in college art education curricula. The problem was not a lack of available design literature. It was a lack of knowledge of design literature among art educators, including professors in college art education programs.

While the Getty enthusiastically promoted its limited fine arts agenda—under theoretical perspectives that ignored issues of "popular" consumer culture, usefulness and usability, and mass production—enrollments in college design programs exploded, making it impossible for art education majors to gain seats in design courses, even as elective study. At the same time, the historic demarcation between fine art and design described in chapter 1 of this text deepened in many schools. Art education and fine arts faculty mistakenly assumed that foundation-level, two- and three-dimensional design classes adequately covered the design fields through exercises in the arrangement of abstract form. Art education emphasis on formal principles, limited exposure to design literature, and little concern for the social consequences of mass-produced objects reinforced some designers' arguments that Bauhaus curricular and pedagogical strategies had disproportionate influence on American art education. Such perceptions also accounted for the poor representation of art educators in the NEA study of design in K–12 classrooms.

Even today, there is resistance among some art educators for K–12 study that is authentic to design thinking, despite the ability of the discipline to connect seamlessly to other subject areas in the K–12 curriculum and overwhelming student interest in the field. Several college art education programs established long-standing commitments to art and design education; however, it is unlikely that most art education majors match enrollment in fine arts courses with comparable study in design. Efforts by the National Art Education Association to expand the domain appear promising, but much of the history of design in K–12 education has developed outside of formal inclusion in fine arts curricula, other than as media-based investigations.

Growing concern over the politicizing of national content standards and the corresponding expansion of standardized testing tempered enthusiasm for curricular experimentation by raising the stakes for teachers under an increasingly narrow definition of student achievement (Davis & Littlejohn, 2016). In 2001, the *No Child Left Behind Act* further accelerated the influence of testing on pedagogy in many states. While there was no widespread belief that students in design-based classrooms did less well on such tests, there was almost no statistical evidence that compared student performance before and after exposure to a design-based pedagogy. A few teachers tracked and showed improvement in standardized test scores by students in design-based classrooms—especially by students in the lower performing quartiles—but this evidence could be attributed by a counting-and-measuring culture to a handful of exceptional teachers.[1] The consequences of developing an approach to teaching and learning through individual, unsystematic experimentation soon became apparent.

In the absence of formal preparation of K-12 educators in design, universities, museums, and professional associations expanded their interest in design education by developing a number of formal and informal learning opportunities for students and teachers. Summer and after-school design camps, such as those at North Carolina State University and Parsons New School of Design, provide precollege preparation for students hoping to become design, professionals when they graduate from four-year universities. These programs allow secondary students to test their interest and aptitude in design before committing to a college major but are seen less as general education in design thinking for students who will not pursue the discipline as a major in college.

The Cooper Hewitt National Design Museum and NC State University develop teachers' abilities to deliver design content and to use the pedagogy of design education in teaching other K-12 subjects. The Cooper Hewitt's program is one of the most enduring, and its funding sources mandate continuous evaluation. The focus of such evaluation, however, is largely on the

---

1. Sixth-grade teachers Leslie Stoltz and Mark Lantz at Chaparral Middle School in Walnut Valley Unified School District (California) compared the standardized test scores of students who enrolled in a traditional classroom for their fifth-grade studies with their scores after completion of a design-based year in their sixth-grade studies (Nelson, D). Scores for four quartiles were compared on the fifth- and sixth-grade Stanford Achievement tests (in Math, Reading, and Language). In all quartiles, students improved their performance from the fifth to sixth grade, although gains by students in the first two quartiles were modest. These were likely students who excel under any teaching strategy. Improvement by students in the last two quartiles, however, was dramatic in all three subjects. When the 2006–2009 test scores of these students were compared to students in traditional classrooms for the three years from the sixth to eighth grade, students who studied under a design-based approach continued to show improvement in their performance on standardized tests at levels beyond that of their traditional classmates. http://www.cpp.edu/~dnelson/intro.html

success of teacher professional development, rather than on the achievement of students against the disciplinary criteria measured by schools. The Cooper Hewitt publishes lectures and teacher-authored lesson plans on the Educators Resource Center portion of the museum's website.

Efforts by professional associations to promote design education have been intermittent, moving in and out of fashion with the interests of changing leadership or a committed practitioner. Such programs generally make students aware of the design professions and issues of the built world but show less interest in facilitating instruction across disciplines. The Chicago Architecture Foundation and the American Architecture Foundation, for example, established the Architecture + Design Education Network (A+DEN) in 2005 to connect teachers to architecture programs throughout the country. Like the Cooper Hewitt, A+DEN publishes teacher lesson plans.

A number of design firms have demonstrated interest in K-12 education, most notably IDEO, the Palo Alto–based design and innovation consulting firm. In addition to working with education clients, the firm publishes its popular *Design Thinking Toolkit for Educators* and collaborates closely with the REDLab (Research in Education and Design Lab) at the Stanford Graduate School of Education, which conducts research on the value of design thinking for teaching and learning.

In recent years, government and nonprofit organizations have turned their attention to preparing an innovative workforce for the future. In 2006, the National Academy of Engineering developed standards for student performance in engineering design and technology in K-12 schools. These standards formed the framework of the 2014 National Assessment of Educational Progress in Technology and Engineering Literacy (TEL), a test of eighth-grade students under the supervision of the National Center for Educational Statistics and National Assessment Governing Board. Commonly described as the Nation's Report Card, NAEP tests began in 1990 as an attempt to define a nationally representative yardstick for assessing over time what American students know and are able to do in various subjects (Davis & Littlejohn, 2016). The TEL test used scenario-based challenges related to Design and Systems, as well as insights regarding Technology and Society and skills related to Information and Communication Technology. None of the tasks required prior scientific or mathematical knowledge. They tested applied problem-solving in the use and design of technology, and for the first time in national testing, all sections of the test were delivered digitally.

The National Center for Educational Statistics reported the TEL test results in June 2016. Some outcomes were surprising; others were predictable. Girls did better than boys, particularly on tasks related to Information and Communication Technology. It is not clear whether girls actually excelled over boys in the use of technology or whether the scenario-based format of the test better suited girls' learning strategies than the typical theory-driven pedagogy of science classrooms. Students in the suburbs generally did better than their counterparts in urban schools where there was less access to technology and instruction. Overall, 43 percent of students performed at or above the proficient level, indicating there is much work to be done in curriculum development.

The TEL test confirmed great variation in where students acquired their knowledge of technology and design. Disturbingly, students attributed only 13 percent of their learning in how to design or fix things to schools. In other words, it appears that K–12 schools are not meeting the national demand for innovation in applied fields such as engineering and that learning depends disproportionately on ad hoc instruction at home. This finding also suggests that the pedagogical emphasis on teaching theory (analytical skills) in higher education described by Avvistati et al. in their 2013 study begins much earlier in students' academic careers.

Finally, nonprofit organizations, such as the MacArthur Foundation through its Digital Media and Learning initiative, have explored the potential of design in education reform. The MacArthur-funded Quest to Learn schools, for example, deliver instruction through design-based challenges and systems thinking using digital technology and game design. MacArthur support of the report *Connected Minds: Technology and Today's Learners* argues that more rigorous research is required to understand the impact of technology use, and by implication design, on today's students (OECD, 2012, p. 167). And most recently, the Organization for Economic Cooperation and Development (OECD) convened two panels in Paris for the development of international rubrics for evaluating critical and creative thinking in K–12 schools and higher education. The application of design thinking plays an important role in all of these initiatives.

Because the history of work in K–12 schools developed largely through isolated, short-term efforts, not through focused research studies or long-term government initiatives, there is little consensus regarding issues necessary to gain consideration of design issues in the preservice education of teachers. Although the NAEP study brings some clarity to engineering-related standards and the OECD work on rubrics looks promising, much is missing in

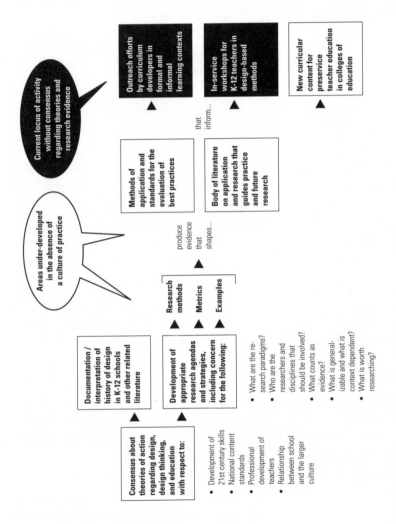

FIGURE 6.4 *Current locus of work in design-based K-12 education.*

terms of theories of action and metrics for measuring knowledge and skills (Figure 6.4: Davis & Littlejohn, 2016). Research that requires participation of minor students, access to their academic records, and intervention in existing curricula for validation is increasingly difficult in today's school cultures. Progress will require organized, collaborative efforts among schools, research institutions, and government agencies that hold promise for systemic change.

THE APPLICATION OF DESIGN TO TEACHING
AND LEARNING IN HIGHER EDUCATION

Calls for developing aptitudes associated with design are not restricted to K-12 education. There is growing concern over how well higher education prepares students in the critical and creative thinking necessary for success in the contemporary workplace and global innovation. The studies described earlier in this chapter show an increasing gap between the output of colleges and universities and the demands of innovation centers worldwide.

Studies also show that students in higher education are generally unprepared for critical and creative thinking and that freshmen arrive at colleges overly confident in their own thinking skills. King and Kitchener report that first-year college students score relatively low on scales of reflective judgment and believe that "absolute truth is only temporarily inaccessible" (King & Kitchener, 1994, p. 224; NC State University, 2014). Freshmen also believe that most problems are well structured and have a high degree of certainty embedded in their definition. When confronted with situations that are ill resolved or uncertain, "they fall back on believing what they want to believe" rather than applying critical inquiry to gain greater clarity about the problem (King & Kitchener, 1994, p. 224). Therefore, researchers recommend engaging students in ambiguous problems from the very start of their college experiences to undermine these tendencies.

Research by the College Board indicates that 80 percent of college-bound seniors graduate from high schools with fewer than five hundred students but enter colleges with enrollments of ten thousand or more (Cuseo, 2007). Educator Karen Spear described the problems in placing first-year students in large enrollment courses that focus on memorization, rather than in interactive learning environments with high expectations that facilitate their transition to college. She warned of the consequences, saying that in such courses students ". . . learn what it is to be a student, what is required to get by. If students are taught to be passive seekers and transcribers of information, that is what they become. Further, they set their sights accordingly in subsequent courses, often actively resisting our attempts in upper-division courses to get them to go beyond the information we give them" (Spear, 1984, pp. 6–7).

Therefore, research suggests delivering some portion of a college education through practice-based instruction that encourages students' critical and creative thinking, regardless of their disciplinary major. The problem, however, is that most college professors were hired for their disciplinary expertise, not for their teaching skills. Few have any formal education in teaching or engagement with an institutional center for teaching effectiveness. And many argue that there is simply too much disciplinary content to cover to add new competencies, not realizing that the development of students' critical and creative thinking is less about what they teach than about how they teach. As a result, most college faculty limit their teaching to the very kind of instruction (i.e. lectures) that research describes as shortchanging the development of students' critical and creative-thinking skills.

NC State University is currently engaged in improving students' critical and creative thinking across the curriculum. Titled THINK!, the five-year study trains faculty in pedagogies that borrow heavily from design education. The first two years of implementation involved more than two thousand freshmen and seventy-six faculty in general education courses, while the remaining three years explore vertical integration of critical and creative thinking in the upper-level curricula of specific disciplinary majors. Participating faculty undergo a week of training and require at least one creative assignment in their syllabi, evaluating results against a common rubric and student reflection. Pre- and post-tests of critical thinking measure student progress. To date, the greatest student gains in critical and creative thinking development have been in large lecture courses where previous pedagogical strategies favored passive listening and memorization. The study is compelling evidence that faculty, when presented with concrete teaching strategies, can adapt design approaches to disciplinary content to achieve the higher-order thinking skills demanded by a knowledge economy.

SUMMARY

The changing nature of the workplace calls for innovation skills and exerts new demands on education. Students arrive in college programs, unprepared for the critical and creative thinking necessary for high-wage employment in innovation jobs. While traditional teaching methods fall short in developing these skills, transfer of the pedagogy of design to K-12 and college classrooms shows promise in achieving the goals of a twenty-first-century education.

There is a long history of using design as a teaching and learning strategy in K-12 schools; however, there is little integration of these methods in the preservice education of classroom teachers. Studies show that K-12 teachers learn about design through informal associations with design professionals and often work in isolation, without colleagues who adopt a design-based approach to teaching and learning. In the United States, evaluation of design-based strategies has been mostly through anecdotal accounts of teachers, although the United Kingdom has been more systematic in its approach to assessment. National and state content standards in the United States in a variety of disciplines serve as entry points for design in K-12 curricula. Rather than introducing new content in an already full course of study, proponents of design-based instruction in the United States advocate using design as a delivery system for any content.

Studies of college teaching and learning show a significant gap between what institutions produce and the skills demanded by high-wage employment. Pedagogical strategies at the college level favor analysis and domain expertise rather than creative synthesis and situated learning. At the same time, faculty report a lack of preparation for teaching critical and creative skills.

CHAPTER 7:
PEDAGOGICAL STRATEGIES FOR TEACHING
THROUGH DESIGN

The instructional strategies described in this chapter have origins in design education and professional design practice. They are long-standing ways of doing things that contribute to the critical and creative thinking of graduates of design programs. The premise underpinning this chapter is that if design programs achieve the outcomes described as essential to a twenty-first-century education, then the signature pedagogy of design education may be useful in reforming teaching and learning in other subject areas.

It is important to recognize that few K-12 curricula have room for new content. Teachers are accountable for student achievement of competencies described in local, state, and national standards. The goal in this discussion is not to teach students to be designers but instead to think like designers—to use design-based strategies as ways of teaching and learning any subject matter or skill. For art teachers who want to qualify students for entry to college design programs or to develop visual problem-solving skills, discussions in Part I of this book may be more satisfying. The examples provided in descriptions of the following instructional strategies begin with an actual content standard for which they are appropriate. Evaluation of student learning outcomes, therefore, is based largely on achieving the competency described in the standard and/or developing overarching critical and creative-thinking skills that are not content dependent.

While the specific examples that follow describe learning activities for K-12 students, the strategies are also successful in teaching college students. As chapter 6 of this book explains, active, project-based approaches to college instruction are likely to produce the critical and creative skills valued by inno-vation companies. Any of these strategies may be adjusted to the level and content of undergraduate students.

The limitations of this book prevent an exhaustive inventory of pedagog-ical strategies. The following examples provide a range of possibilities, with many alternatives in common practice in college-level design programs.

SCENARIOS

A scenario is a script for action. It presents a situated, goal-oriented challenge or problem through a story or narrative. Nesting the story within a specific setting invites students to make critical inferences from relevant information and to project the consequences of actions taken to resolve the challenge. As a concept, the scenario dates from the Italian Renaissance practice of pinning written notes to the back of stage scenery that described the characters, plot, and actions for an improvisational performance. Today, scenarios are used to guide problem-solving in a number of fields, including technology and busi-ness. Following is a list of the components of the strategy.

Challenge

A scenario challenge illustrates a concept, principle, or method that is trans-ferrable to similar situations. Constraints in the challenge often compete with each other, requiring students' critical judgment in reconciling opposing pri-orities. The challenge may require application of prior knowledge—such as content acquired through a reading assignment, findings gathered through research, or skills learned in other contexts—or it may depend entirely on explicit or implicit information provided by the scenario description.

Context

The physical, psychological, technological, social/cultural, and economic con-ditions relevant to the challenge comprise the context of the scenario. In some cases, the task for students is to decide how many contextual factors they can address—to first frame the problem or challenge in ways that are manage-able and justifiable. Aspects of the context interact, requiring conjecture about possible consequences of paying more attention to some than others.

For example, if the challenge is to design a "fish taxi" for transporting a goldfish from the pet store to home while riding a bicycle with both hands, the general condition for fish survival is known and unchangeable: continual immersion in a sufficient supply of clean water. However, the movement caused by pedaling a bicycle makes some materials and sizes less desirable than others in containing water and shielding the fish from impact with the bicycle frame. Securing the "taxi" to the human body may be a better solution than attaching it to the bicycle. Students, therefore, must identify how much of the context is relevant to the challenge, interdependencies among competing factors, and importance assigned to each factor in meeting the challenge.

The context may be familiar to students, easily accessible for observation, or from a time and place in the past or future. Shifting a familiar challenge to an unfamiliar setting or removing obvious options—for example, a plastic bag for the fish taxi—often calls into question popular conventions.

Stakeholders

Stakeholders are all the people or entities involved in the activity or setting described by the scenario, including those necessary to maintain the system. The scope of the problem or scale of the surrounding context determines who is a stakeholder. The fish taxi certainly requires consideration for the needs of the fish but also for the cyclist and maybe the pet store clerk as well. Students must abandon personal preferences and imagine what is useful, usable, and desirable to others.

Activities

Activities are the means through which stakeholders interact with the context. Students may create a suitable environment for a fish, but the activity of riding a bicycle introduces aspects to the challenge not present if the scenario simply described walking home from the pet store. Activities suggest additional criteria for evaluating options.

Goals

Stakeholders have motives for interacting with the context that are stated explicitly or implicitly in the scenario. There is a preferred outcome for each stakeholder that satisfies the most constraints or the most important constraints. While there is always more than one right solution to a challenge, an articulated goal establishes the criteria by which outcomes will be judged. It is important for students to think beyond the attributes of products and define goals in terms of the conditions or experiences they produce.

The narrative describing a scenario must be sufficiently detailed so that students can make inferences from the available information without consulting the faculty. Students' ability to make and justify such inferences—abductive reasoning—is among the transferrable skills faculty evaluate. The description should also include facts that are germane to the challenge and others that are not, so faculty can assess students' discrimination between relevant and irrelevant information as a part of the overall evaluation. When possible, several factors should require students to apply values in weighting the importance of satisfying some constraints over others. Finally, the scenario should allow for a range of appropriate solutions.

Scenario Example

A Connecticut elementary school standard asks students to: *identify basic needs and wants and, through example, explain why people cannot have everything they want* (National History Education Clearinghouse, 2016). The scenario designed to address this standard describes three people residing at a research station in the North Pole: a sixty-year-old female climate scientist, a thirty-year-old male journalist for a scientific magazine, and a young research assistant (the student). It describes the work-related tasks for which each person is responsible and leisure-time activities preferred by the team members. It also provides details of the setting: zero daylight hours between October and December; average annual temperature of 32°F with a record low of -45°; average wind speeds of ten to fifteen miles per hour with gusts as high as fifty miles per hour; and no fish on the sea bed or vegetation. Polar bears don't travel this far north.

The challenge is to outfit the station, spending no more than one hundred points from the list in Figure 7.1. The points assigned to each item on the list depend on faculty rankings against a particular value system (comfort versus survival; individual versus group needs; or work versus leisure activities), but the one-hundred-point total makes it impossible to acquire everything on the list. Students begin by generating a series of questions they would ask each

FIGURE 7.1 *Outfitting a polar research station.*

Enough heat to keep rooms at 72º	xx points
Enough heat ro keep rooms at 62º	xx points
Individual bedrooms (requires more energy to heat)	xx points
Gas powered stove	xx points
Refrigerator	xx points
Windows	xx points/window
Thermal draperies	xx points/window
Washing machine	xx points
Clothes dryer	xx points
Flat screen TV	xx points/hour
PlayStation	xx points/hour
DVD player	xx points/hour
Computer time	xx points/hour
Printer	xx points/hour
Light during hours of dark	xx points/hour
Exercise bicycle	xx points
All-terrain vehicle	xx points

member of the research team to determine their individual needs and wants. They then construct a "shopping list" and justify their choices of items. The list requires trade-offs. A student may be willing to maintain a slightly lower room temperature to gain leisure time on the computer. The list also includes items that may be of interest to only one resident of the station or irrelevant to the work-related tasks. If there is no daylight during the months of residence, windows are unnecessary and contribute to heat loss. A refrigerator may not be necessary in a climate with temperatures at freezing or below. Students present their lists to the class.

Faculty can evaluate any scenario-based activity in terms of the following criteria.

- Did students assess relevant information regarding the context and challenge goal? Could they analyze information provided by the narrative or additional reading and make inferences about aspects of the context that contributed to the solution?
- Did their solutions to the challenge acknowledge the motives of various stakeholders and range of activities related to their tasks? Could they identify constraints and opportunities related to these factors?

- Did they reach well-reasoned conclusions, openly considering alternative points of view?
- Did they effectively communicate the analysis of the problem and rationale for proposed solutions to others?

PERSONAS

Personas are fictional characters or composites based on real people who stand in for different types of stakeholders in a scenario. They embody the motives, values, and behaviors of hypothetical groups of people in some targeted activity. Marketers use personas to understand the motives of particular consumers. Software designers use personas to anticipate the actions of specific users. Personas put real faces on abstract data and overcome the tendency to generalize "average" participants without understanding specific wants and needs.

IDEO partner Fred Dust describes research for a luxury client involving an interview and observation of a middle-age woman. When asked about her engagement with luxury items and services, she professed leading a very simple life with no interest in such things. However, observation revealed she had a standing appointment at a nail salon. When asked about this, she argued that this was not self-indulgence but an *essential* service. In other words, her definition of "luxury" was not the same as that of the designers. The observation was necessary to overcome the ambiguity of language in the interview and to understand the real behavior of users. In many cases, designers describe personas in terms of "extreme users," believing they will meet the needs and wants of the average person by satisfying individuals at the two ends of some continuum of values or experience.

Designers frequently produce short videos explaining the behaviors and beliefs of various stakeholders. They often follow design work with similar videos demonstrating solutions in use so that others understand the implications for various people. Asking students to make such media presentations requires them to see things literally through the eyes of another.

It is particularly difficult for students to empathize with perspectives other than their own. Limited life experience tends to reinforce existing attitudes and assumptions. Role-playing the position of different personas can illustrate multiple viewpoints on an event or task. It gives students "permission" to act in ways different from their own natural behavior, thereby experiencing firsthand an alternate position on an issue, event, or activity. A typical example in the field of architecture is to ask a student to navigate a complex environment in a wheelchair or blindfolded. The graded or uneven walkway that they take for granted becomes an exhausting challenge. Talking with people from a seated position or without facial cues is disorienting. Such understanding is rarely understood through abstract descriptions.

Persona Example

North Carolina social studies standards call for middle school students to understand *how the development of infrastructure, such as roads, canals, and railroads changed North Carolina communities.* In addition, North Carolina students are to learn *how African slave labor contributed to the development and organization of plantations* (North Carolina Department of Public Instruction, 2013). Middle school social studies teacher Chuck Hennessy had difficulty motivating his students to read required textbook descriptions of colonial life in North Carolina related to this standard. He devised a scenario around an obscure colonial law that required every North Carolina citizen in the 1700s to devote four days a year to road building. He gave students a map (Figure 7.2) and divided the class into four groups: small farmers, town merchants, plantation owners, and the town council. The map illustrated a river and dock through which goods flowed in and out of the community and a section of road that had been built during the previous year. The current year's road building could continue the route to the town and businesses, to small farms, or almost but not quite to the plantation. Each group of students constructed an oral argument for continuation of the road in a particular direction with an ultimate decision on the route by the town council.

The role-playing activity illustrates several important issues:

- The competitive role-playing aspect of the assignment is highly motivating for middle school students. They want the town council to choose their recommended route. However, students cannot construct successful arguments without supporting detail. They must return to the textbook for information that validates their position— the types of goods the community imported and exported, the contribution of those goods to economic prosperity, the power structure

FIGURE 7.2 *Role-playing activity.*

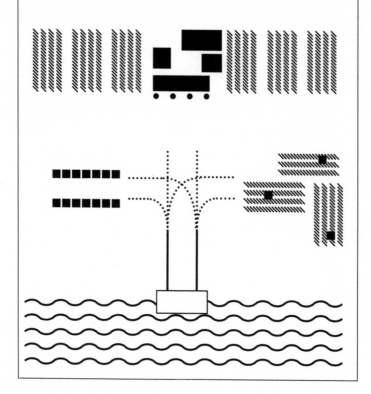

Colonial North Carolina law required every citizen to devote four days a year to roadbulding. Student groups adopt personas in advocating for one of three possible routes the road could take from the dock on the river: to the town and shops of merchants; to small farms; or almost but not quite to the plantations. Students construct logical arguments for presentation to the town council, based on information in their textbook reading assignments.

of the culture—now evaluating content within the context of a personal mission.

• The activity requires the construction and presentation of a logical argument. Students must determine what information is relevant to their argument through a process of critical thinking. They structure information as a sequence of connected statements that establish a proposition: premises or reasons for accepting the argument; more detailed propositions inferred from the available information; and conclusions.

- There are competing values embedded within the activity. The plantation owners represent a disproportionate impact on the economics of the community, yet to continue the road to the plantation (further than can be built in one year), they will need to use slaves.
- The activity shows that there can be multiple perspectives on a single issue, all backed by justifications that have their bases in facts. The use of personas develops student empathy for these various positions.

Beyond meeting these specific content standards, there are a number of important questions faculty can ask when evaluating students' performance:

- Did students structure arguments that logically led to stated conclusions?
- Were statements that comprised the arguments clear, accurate, precise, and relevant?
- Did students support arguments with information from the text and inferences from the map?
- Were arguments particular to the assigned personas, and did they anticipate alternate arguments from competing groups? Could they generate creative solutions that overcame the inherent limitations of their recommendation?

ANALOGICAL THINKING

Analogical thinking uses information from one source to tackle a creative challenge in another. This type of thinking "makes the strange familiar" by comparing something unknown to something known and "makes the familiar strange" by comparing a known thing to something seemingly unrelated. Research shows that creative people in many fields are highly analogical in their thinking. For example, scientist Friedrich Kekulé said he discovered the ring formation of benzene by daydreaming of a snake chasing its tail. George de Mestral invented Velcro after noticing when walking his dog that the prickly seeds of the Burdock plant attached themselves to the dog's fur.

Analogies depend on correspondences, distinct relationships between two things. One type of analogy addresses *physical* similarities: a door is like the cover of a book, hinged on one side, open on the other. A second type of analogy shows a *conceptual* correspondence: the eyes are windows to the soul.

A third type shows a *system* correspondence: the internal structure of the atom is like the planets orbiting around the sun. Designers use these types of analogies in solving an array of problems. Apple Inc., for example, studied concierge services in luxury hotels when designing the service system for its commercial stores. An Apple employee greets customers and directs them to the appropriate staff and areas of the store that meet their needs.

Analogical Thinking Example

Grade-three Common Core English Language Arts Standards ask students to *describe characters in a story (e. g., their traits, motivations, or feelings) and explain how their actions contribute to the sequence of events* (Common Core State Standards Initiative, 2016). The task is to develop a heroic character for a fictional story. Students generally rely on stereotypes from contemporary media. The first activity is to list all of the predictable characteristics that are associated with the stereotype. The teacher then asks a series of questions that encourage students to expand the characteristics (Gordon, 1973).

- What if the hero were a machine? What kind of machine would he/she be and what machine-like characteristics would he/she exhibit?
- Can you think of an analogy in the animal world that would describe a kind of behavior or activity in which the hero might engage? How might you use this information to communicate something about the hero's personality?

Students then generate situations in which the hero finds him/herself and discuss how the character's response is an extension of the machine or animal analogy.

Analogies can also encourage students to communicate more descriptively, to deepen meaning by comparing something to another experience in some detail. A writing or visual exercise might ask students to build analogies to activities or experiences by describing something that is like:

- Starting classes in a new school
- Having an argument with a close friend
- Winning a contest
- Learning to ride a bicycle
- Getting a new pet

Similarly, advanced students can build analogies to concepts in a range of disciplines. In this activity, students describe the relationships or conditions in the first half of sentences by generating analogies in the second half of sentences. Students then justify their responses through details of the comparisons. This activity is evaluative and lets the teacher know how well students truly understand the event, process, or phenomenon in the lesson.

- The body's conversion of food to energy is like ...
- The formation of a thunderstorm is like ...
- The invasion of Poland in World War II was like ...
- The democratic form of government is like ...

VISUALIZATION

Earlier discussions in this book build a case for developing students' visual/spatial thinking along with their literacy and numeracy. Robert McKim described flexibility in moving among vehicles of thought—numbers, language, and visual images—as fundamental to creative work. The US Department of Labor Secretary's Commission on Necessary Skills identified "seeing things in the mind's eye" as an essential thinking competency for productive work in the twenty-first century. The Knowledgeworks Foundation—in its *2020 Forecast: Creating the Future of Learning*—discussed "new forms of sense-making" as shaping success in the knowledge economy (Knowledgeworks, 2008). National Voluntary Content Standards in the Language Arts addressed interpreting "nonprint" media—such as film, charts and diagrams, and photographs—as an essential skill.

Schools dedicate considerable time to developing students' computational and linguistic abilities but very little time on visual literacy. When visual matters enter the curriculum, it is usually through the arts where issues of self-expression, mastery of materials, and craft often dominate concerns for clarity and appropriateness. And although a number of disciplines ask students to read visual presentations of information, very few are sufficiently critical of how and what students make as representations of information.

Simply making something visual doesn't ensure that students will be critical in their visual choices. Richard Saul Wurman, in his book *Information Anxiety*, argued that there is no lack of information in today's media-rich environment. What we lack is understanding. He claimed that there are really only five ways to organize information in charts and diagrams: by alphabet, category, time, location, and continuum. Yet this is something rarely explained to students or demonstrated by comparing the same information in different forms. As a result, students lack critical frameworks for evaluating the patterns that emerge from these various representational strategies.

Cognitive psychologist Donald Norman argues that there are principles for making choices among ways of visualizing information. His *appropriateness principle* suggests that qualities of representations be appropriate to the specific task at hand (Norman, 1993). For example, the US Department of Agriculture Food Pyramid (1992–2005) asked consumers to consider a balanced diet by comparing differently sized wedges of a polyhedron that represented various food groups. However, we don't make nutritional decisions on the basis of volume or surface area. Instead, we plan meals in terms of the number of daily servings: three to five servings of vegetables, two to three servings of meat, poultry, and fish. In this case, the numbers and language that appeared outside the visual diagram were much more useful in making nutritional choices than a visual representation of volume. On the other hand, if we want to understand patterns in water movement off the coast of the United States, we will probably have a better sense of the speed and direction of currents if we represent the data collected by hundreds of tiny sensors as fluttering underwater flags than as a table of numbers.

Norman's *perceptual principle* states that the perceptual qualities of a visual representation should match the properties of the data (Norman, 1993). To show the size of voter turnout in each of the fifty states, for example, it makes sense to code each state with a single color that deepens in value (from light to dark) with increasing percentages of voters, rather than to use random patterns or colors. While readers may not immediately recognize exact percentages without consulting the legend, they will be able to identify states with the highest turnouts. The goal in visualizing data, therefore, is to reveal patterns that are more difficult (or impossible) to interpret in numerical or linguistic form. Imagine representing voter turnout as an alphabetical listing of states followed by numbers. It is possible to make comparisons from state to state but not to understand patterns of participation across the country.

Designers use visualization strategies to bring form to hazy impressions, to model possible solutions to complex problems, and to communicate ideas to others. There are a number of visualization strategies that can be effective in a variety of classroom applications:

- Modeling and diagramming
- Concept mapping
- Storyboarding

Modeling and Diagramming

Modeling is a visualization strategy that uses visual/spatial language to illustrate physical and conceptual relationships. Models are important because they both reflect and shape our perceptions of things. Figure 7.3 shows two models for depicting global geography as a flat map. The top map is the sixteenth-century Mercator Projection, the most common flattened view of the Earth. The projection distorts land area to favor east/west ocean navigation. Connecting two points on the map indicates the sailing direction. The bottom map is the Peters Projection, developed in 1973 to show actual land mass relationships. Both maps are accurate within their respective mathematical models, but they differ in intent and the conclusions they support. It is easy to imagine that the Mercator Projection influences policy decisions in favor of northern hemisphere countries, which appear proportionately larger than they actually are.

Schools typically engage students in *reading* models and diagrams but less so in *making* them and the constructivist thinking that such making involves. And the types of models that schools do assign often ask students to replicate the physical properties of things while ignoring other kinds of relationships that can be expressed spatially. Students spend hours recreating the thatching on a model of Shakespeare's 1599 Globe Theatre, never understanding the influence of the architecture on the relationship between performer and audience.

Diagrams are simplified drawings that illustrate the structure of something—schematics that capture in visual form the essential relationships among elements or ideas. There are many types of diagrams and each holds potential for revealing particular kinds of information. A Venn diagram, for example, shows overlapping territory among elements, while a flow chart shows elements in time and infers cause/effect relationships not present in the Venn. At a time when software can put any kind of information into a pie chart—regardless of whether it truly describes a parts-to-whole relationship—moving flexibly among diagrammatic types that are appropriate to the task is an important critical-thinking skill.

FIGURE 7.3 *Mercator (top) and Peters (bottom) Projections.*

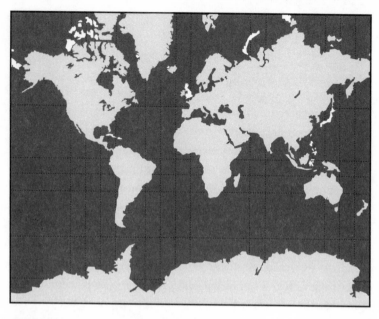

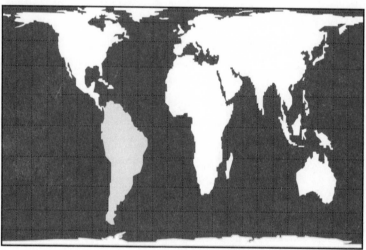

The purpose of modeling and diagramming activities, therefore, is not merely to share information with others but to think through making. Models and diagrams function as cognitive artifacts that allow students to manipulate more information than can be processed only in the mind, yet schools spend very little time on development of these skills.

Modeling Example

New York City Social Studies Standards ask students to *explain how events are related chronologically to one another . . . recognize the dynamics of historical continuity and change over periods of time . . . and use periods of time to put events in chronological order* (NYC Department of Education, 2015).

The following example requires small groups of students to model an abstract concept: change in the American family since 1900. The only material used is newspaper, and students may not rely on photographs, text, or tools to develop their models. They should imagine the newspaper as blank. After twenty minutes, students stop working and explain their model to another group. A variation of this assignment introduces new information ten minutes into the process, allowing students to adjust their models on the basis of new facts before presentation. US Bureau of Statistics data on births to teenage mothers, marriages, and divorces, for example, can undercut student assumptions about the instability of contemporary families.

The modeling activity illustrates a number of important outcomes:

- The assignment asks students to model an abstract concept (in this case, change). The material (newspaper) is so crude that it is impossible to make elements that physically resemble what they stand for with any detail. Differences in size may indicate age or gender, but students spend no time on physical replication. Effort goes toward defining meaningful concepts and patterns in data, not things.

- Small groups begin the activity through conversation and negotiation, with members sharing what they know about the topic. In this way, students reveal assumptions and biases about prior knowledge before they commit to visualizing concepts. This makes the activity particularly useful as a prelude to a writing assignment or a debate on social issues.

- Typically, the model evolves through ongoing conversation, supported by quick demonstration of formal possibilities as explanations to peers. Someone makes something and others react, changing or elaborating the original form through discussion. Unlike traditional modeling in schools, there is little physical investment in creating well-crafted form, so students are willing to reconsider or even abandon early attempts based on negotiation with peers.

- There are no "good or bad" paper crumplers. In many traditional modeling activities, students with strong craft skills dominate activity and less skilled partners sit back and watch. The material in this activity evens the playing field among students.

- In many K–12 learning activities, students' demonstration of what they know is held hostage by writing or public speaking. Regardless of the nature of the knowledge, students must demonstrate competency through a verbal filter. Modeling and diagramming provide insight into what students know and are able to do without this filter. For example, the student who locates small balls of newspaper on a large flat rectangle illustrates that the number of children in early twentieth-century families had some relationship to farm acreage the family had to cultivate. He may not be able to articulate that concept fully in writing or recognize it in a test question, but when prompted to explain the model, he is capable of describing what he made and why.

- Typically, the models generated by different groups show a range of visualization strategies. Some build timelines, others construct constellation diagrams, and others create categorical typologies. This diversification opens discussions regarding different interpretations of the same information and the pattern each type of model reveals.

- Because faculty are not seen as sources of information for the activity, they are free to eavesdrop on conversations.

Concept Mapping

Concept maps illustrate meaningful relationships among concepts; two or more concept nodes are linked by words or phrases to form a proposition regarding the nature of the relationship. They make clear the structural position of various elements within a system or the hierarchy of ideas in a conceptual landscape.

Concept maps are also useful in organizing and revealing patterns in content delivered through another method. Studies show that note taking by most students is a continuous but undifferentiated recording of information as presented in lectures or textbooks. Few students go back to process their notes in ways that reveal cause-effect relationships, delineate significant patterns, challenge underlying assumptions, or describe leverage points where key decisions or events are responsible for outcomes. Concept maps summarize these relationships in visual form, making patterns more apparent.

In other cases, students struggle with writing activities that require the integration of content from multiple sources or the imposition of hierarchy on a collection of ideas. Word-processing software often forces students to commit to a linear narrative before they fully understand the relationships among elements or ideas. On the other hand, nodal concept maps can be entered from any point, allowing students to explore multiple narrative sequences for telling the same story. Students can compare the implications of moving from general-to-specific versus specific-to-general, for example, before they begin writing. They can determine topics that are subsets of larger concepts. They can recognize a tangent or dead end that departs from the major theme or bypasses important issues. In this sense, the visualization of writing allows students to think through alternative narratives in ways that linear verbal outlines do not.

Concept maps are also helpful in framing areas or topics for investigation. They allow students to see the scope of a problem and to scale work realistically. Defining the limits of an independent investigation and maintaining focus on relevant aspects of the problem throughout the duration of an assignment is often difficult for students. Concept maps remind students of the boundaries of their studies—what is included and what is not.

It is often unclear to faculty whether students fully understand the structure of information delivered in lectures or readings. Concept maps reveal students' misperceptions as well as insights. In this way, they are evaluative; they allow faculty to judge student understanding before proceeding to new content.

The main components of a concept mapping activity include:

- *Content*: Students need some familiarity with the subject matter to be mapped, either through previous studies, assigned readings, observational activities, or life experiences.
- *Focusing question*: A focusing question helps students determine the appropriate depth and breadth content in the map and the hierarchy among concepts or elements.
- *Key concepts or elements*: Students list key concepts or elements, clustering related items under larger conceptual categories. They rank items within clusters from general to specific or by some other relevant ordering strategy, such as time or cause-effect relationships. Concepts and elements become nodes in the map, with shapes and sizes

reflecting members of a category and levels of specificity. It is often helpful to generate concepts or elements as individual Post-Its that allow for multiple arrangements within the map as work progresses.

- *Framing sentence*: Students describe the nature of the relationships among elements through overarching sentences that act as armatures for locating concepts and elements within the overall map. A primary framing sentence anchors general categories in spatial locations within the composition. Branching sentences exit from the framing sentence and provide detail.

Concept Mapping Example

The National Academy of Engineering developed standards for K–12 schools that guided the 2014 National Assessment of Educational Progress/Technology and Engineering Literacy, commonly referred to as the Nation's Report Card. The grade-eight standards related to Technology and Society ask students to *realize that the interplay between technology and culture is dynamic . . . to recognize that technology developed for one purpose is later adapted to other purposes . . . and to analyze systems* (National Assessment Governing Board, 2014).

Studies of technological devices often focus on discrete features or functions without considering implications for the breadth of their influence on larger systems and human lives. This activity asks students to place an invention—such as a cell phone, washing machine, radio, or printing press—at the center of the map (Figure 7.4) and to complete the map by adding images and descriptive text that identify particular relationships between the device and its context. Each student investigates a different device but addresses the same propositional structure.

Storyboarding

A storyboard is a sequence of images that allow filmmakers and animators to previsualize movies, games, and animations. It was developed as an imaging strategy at the Walt Disney Studio in the early 1930s and became a common practice in the production of live-action films in the 1940s. Storyboards illustrate camera movement, sounds effects (in notes), and the portion of settings included in any given shot. Today's students have deep experiences with media, and visual storytelling plays an important role in their leisure activities.

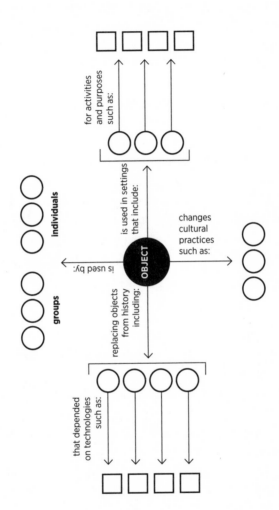

FIGURE 7.4 *Concept mapping the historical, technological, social, and cultural effects of an invention.*

Psychologist Jean Mandler writes in *Stories, Scripts, and Scenes* about recurring mental structures that result in common types of psychological processing. Stories and scripts represent *event schemas*, which are hierarchically organized as episodes and connected parts of a whole. A story is a particular type of schema for which there are expectations about how the narrative will proceed, regardless of the readers' cultural experiences and the specific content of the story. A story structure has a setting; a protagonist who reacts to some event or antagonist in the beginning of the story; a goal that determines the protagonist's path through the story; other characters with which the protagonist interacts along the path; and a concluding event and outcome. Stories are organized temporally or causally (Mandler, 1984, 2009).

Storyboards visualize this recurring structure by ordering the narrative as scenes in ways that writing alone may not. As drawings or collages, each cell of the storyboard demands visual and auditory description that might otherwise be overlooked in other forms of student writing. Storyboards call attention to the structure, over and above the specific content of the story. For this reason, they are helpful in teaching writing.

Storyboarding Example

Common Core Writing Standards require middle school students to *engage and orient the reader by establishing a context and point of view and introducing a narrator and/or characters and organizing an event sequence that unfolds naturally and logically; to use precise words and phrases, telling details, and sensory language to convey a vivid picture of experiences, events, and/or characters* (Common Core State Standards Initiative, 2016).

This example asks students to design the storyboard (Figure 7.5) for a movie about two one-inch characters' journey across the breakfast table. They work on a page of blank cells with lines below for adding verbal description to each scene. They are told to consider actions, lighting, camera angles, and dialogue as well as characters and plot. After completing the storyboard, they are to write the story.

Faculty can evaluate student performance in terms of meeting the standard but also assess the storyboard in terms of the following:

- Do scenes illustrate a clear point of view? How is that point of view achieved visually, and can the student translate this visual description in writing?

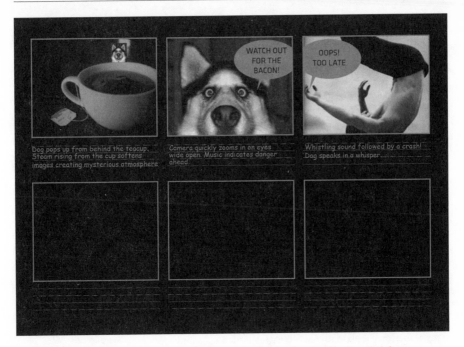

FIGURE 7.5 *A storyboard captures a sequence of events in visual and verbal form.*

- Is there is a discernible structure in the ordering of story events? Do scenes foreshadow or recall other events in the sequence?
- Are scenes described in rich detail, and are students able to substitute figurative language for the quality of visuals in the later writing?

SIMULATIONS AND PROTOTYPES

A *simulation* is an imitation of a real-world process or system behavior over time. Flight simulators, for example, respond to commands from the pilot, much as would real airplanes. A *prototype* is an early sample of a solution to a problem constructed to test the applications of concepts, principles, or properties. Today, many simulations and prototypes are digital. In other cases, they can be crude mockups of physical artifacts or drills for executing plans under proposed conditions. Through the critical and creative testing of simulations and prototypes, designers refine ideas and provide specifications for a real working solution, rather than a theoretical one.

Simulation Example

The Next Generation Science Standards ask high school students *to evaluate merits and limitations of two different models of the same proposed tool, process, mechanism, or system in order to select or revise a model that best fits the evidence or design criteria; to design a test of a model to ascertain its reliability and to develop and/or use multiple types of models to provide mechanistic accounts and/or predict phenomena, and move flexibly between model types based on merits and limitations* (Next Generation Science Standards, 2012).

In this example, ten to fifteen students each remove one shoe and study the treads. They rank the shoes from *least predicted* traction to *most predicted* traction, basing judgments on some articulated theory of what produces traction in shoe design. Using a four-inch-by-five-foot board with a line drawn across the middle, they test each shoe by placing the toe on the line and raising one end of the board until the shoe slides and the toe breaks the line (Figure 7.6). With a yardstick, they measure the height of the board at the moment the shoe begins to slide. Students then compare the results for each shoe, creating a new ranking based on *actual* traction.

FIGURE 7.6 *Simulation test of shoe traction.*

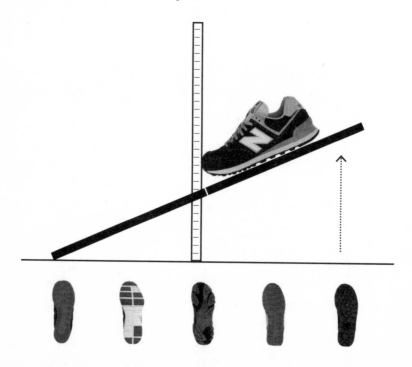

Students are then asked what factors the simulation does not account for (for example, weight, size, materials, momentum, surface conditions) and suggest simulations that would test for these factors. Then they design new shoe treads for various activities—such as tennis, mountain hiking, basketball, etc.—based on their understanding of the effect of all factors on the traction required by each sport.

Faculty can ask a number of general questions in evaluating student performance:

- Can students articulate plausible theories that guide their predictions?
- How clearly, accurately, and precisely do simulations and prototype testing replicate real conditions?
- How relevant are simulations and prototypes in providing insight or demonstrating the significance to the problem at hand?
- How original are the simulation and prototyping testing strategies?
- How rigorous and systematic is the testing procedure?
- Can students adjust their theories based on evidence from simulations and prototype testing?

COMPETING CONSTRAINTS

As discussed in previous chapters, design almost always involves competing constraints. In satisfying one constraint, meeting the demands of another may be compromised. The goal for designers is to address the most important constraints with the fewest negative consequences resulting from not satisfying others. Designers rarely understand all problem constraints at the beginning of work. Some surface through research, and because problem variables are interdependent, addressing one limitation or requirement can produce another concern. In the example that follows, students learn to reconsider early decisions as new requirements emerge.

Competing Constraints Example

A South Carolina elementary-level science standard asks students to *recall the characteristics of an organism's habitat that allow the organism to survive there and to explain how changes in the habitats of plants and animals affect their survival* (South Carolina Department of Education, 2007). The activity scenario describes a young green iguana from Costa Rico who can only stay in the classroom if students can design a home that will keep him healthy, safe, and happy. The activity includes:

- Determining the size of the home
- Selecting the building materials
- Heating the home
- Furnishing the home
- Explaining the thinking behind design decisions

Students receive facts about green iguanas. They weigh two to four pounds and are twenty-eight to thirty-six inches in length. Iguanas are cold-blooded and need to maintain a body temperature of 88° (in air temperatures between 85°–96°), although they bask at higher temperatures when digesting food. They shed their skin every five to eight weeks and need a moist environment. They climb trees and retreat to water when threatened. Their small claws tear easily, so they need soft, smooth surfaces to walk on.

When first asked to determine the size of the home, students find no requirement guiding dimensions other than the mature size of the reptile. Building material options include several gauges of screen mesh, bamboo, sheet metal, rubber matting, and glass. Students infer that material choices affect the retention of water, ease of cleaning the home, visibility of the iguana in his habitat, and protection of his claws. The third task, heating the home, involves the placement of a heating lamp on the perimeter of the structure. Now the size of the home and type of enclosure matters in controlling the heat distribution. Too small or too enclosed and the home exceeds the recommended temperature. Too large or too open and it is impossible to control the temperature beyond the ambient temperature of the classroom. Providing branches for climbing also challenges original decisions regarding the height of the home.

Students are then asked to determine which of the following statements describe their findings:

- The smaller the size of the home, the less variation in temperature in the space.
- The larger the home, the warmer the overall space of the home.
- The placement of the heat lamp determines how much variation in temperature will be found across the space.

- The characteristic behaviors of the reptile influence decisions about the home.
- Building materials should be natural, not man–made.

Because the steps of the activity are sequenced, faculty can assess students' reasoning. Some students will return to original decisions and make changes as new information becomes relevant. Others will complete steps without reconsideration of earlier choices or appear to make random selections among options with no overarching theories about the relationships among variables.

SUMMARY

What the examples illustrate is that design activities move easily across disciplines and support required learning objectives without adding content to an already full curriculum. They engage students in active learning that applies abstract concepts from textbooks and lectures to real-world problems. Faculty need not be experts in design to evaluate student performance, because the questions that drive judgments are based in thinking skills, not in the craftsmanship of artifacts.

REFERENCES

CHAPTER 1

Adams, S. (2013). "The Unpaid Internship Is Not Dead Yet." *Forbes* magazine. June 20, 2013. http://www. forbes. com/sites/susanadams/2013/06/20/the-unpaid-internship-is-not-dead-yet/#4aa17b311a36. Retrieved February 13, 2016.

American Institute of Architects. "The History of the AIA." http://www.aia .org/about/history/AIAB028819. Retrieved February 7, 2016.

Aynsley, J. (2009). *Designing Modern Germany*. London: Reaktion.

Barrett, D. and Martinez, A. eds. (2008). *Infinite Radius: Founding Rhode Island School of Design*. Providence: Rhode Island School of Design.

California College of the Arts. (2016). https://www.cca.edu/about/history.

Chafee, R. (1977). "The Teaching of Architecture at the École des Beaux-Arts." *The Architecture of the École des Beaux-Arts*. Arthur Drexler, ed. Cambridge, MA: Museum of Modern Art and MIT Press.

Cohen, J. A. (1994). "Building a Discipline: Early Institutional Settings for Architectural Education in Philadelphia." *Journal of the Society of Architectural Historians*. Volume 53, Number 2. pp. 139–183.

Cole, H. (1853). Department of Practical Art: Elementary Drawing Schools, 1853, National Training Art School. London: George E. Eyre and William Spottiswood, for Her Majesty's Stationery Office. Cited at: http://sculpture.gla.ac.uk/view/organization.php?id=msib4_1267714397. Retrieved on February 16, 2016.

Crowston, C. (2009). "From School to Workshop: Pre-training and Apprenticeship in Old Regime France." *Learning on the Shop Floor: Historical Perspectives on Apprenticeship*. De Munck, B. et al. eds. New York, NY: Berghahn. pp. 46–60.

Davis, Meredith. (2016). "'Normal Science' and the Changing Practices of Design and Design Education." *Visible Language*. Volume 50, Number 1.

Davis, Meredith, Dubberly, H., Evenson, S., and Laurel, B. (2001). *Developing Curricula for Experience Design*. AIGA and the National Association of Schools of Art and Design.

Davis, Meredith, Hawley, P., and Spilka, G. (1997). *Design as a Catalyst for Learning*. Alexandria, VA: Association for Supervision and Curriculum Development.

Davis, Michael. (2010). "Distinguishing between Architects and Engineers." *Philosophy and Engineering: An Emerging Agenda.* Ibo van de Poel and David Goldberg, eds. New York, NY: Springer. pp. 15–31.

De Angeli Walls, N. (2001). *Art, Industry, and Women's Education in Philadelphia.* Westport, CT: Bergin & Garvey.

Droste, M. (2006). *Bauhaus 1919–1933.* London: Taschen.

Dubberly, H. (2005). *How Do You Design?* Funded by grant from Sun Microsystems. Available as a pdf at: http://www. dubberly.com/articles/how-do-you-design.html.

Dubberly, H. and Rith, C. (2007). "Why Horst W. J. Rittel Matters." *Design Issues,* Volume 23, Number 1, Winter 2007. pp. 72–91.

Efland, A. (1990). *A History of Art Education: Intellectual and Social Currents in Teaching the Visual Arts.* New York, NY: Teachers College Press.

Esptein, S. (1998). "Craft Guilds, Apprenticeship, and Technological Change in Pre-industrial Europe." *Journal of Economic History.* Volume 58, Number 3. September 1998. pp. 684–713.

Fjord. (2015). Retrieved in April 2016 from the web at: https://www.Accenture.com/t20150709T045835_w_us-en/_acnmedia/Accenture/Conversation-Assets/Microsites/Documents14/Accenture-Fjord-Trends-2015.pdf.

Fricker, D. and Fricker, J. (2010). *The Beaux Arts Style.* Baton Rouge, LA: Louisiana Division of Historic Preservation.

Gantz, C. (2015). "History of IDSA: IDSA and Its Predecessors." http://www.idsa.org/history-idsa. Retrieved February 7, 2016.

Gerbino, A. (2010). *François Blondell: Architecture, Erudition, and the Scientific Revolution.* London: Routledge.

Heller, S. (1993). "Cult of the Ugly." *Eye* magazine. Volume 3, Number 9. Retrieved from *Eye* digital archives on February 7, 2016 at: http://www.eyemagazine.com/feature/article/cult-of-the-ugly.

Heller, S. and Gluck, N. (1989). "Seventy-five years of AIGA." http://www.aiga.org/about-history-75thanniversary/. Retrieved February 7, 2016.

Heslop, T. A. (1997). "How Strange the Change from Major to Minor: Hierarchies and Medieval Art." *The Culture of Craft.* P. Dormer, ed. New York, NY: Manchester University Press.

Interior Designers for Legislation in New York. http://www.idlny.org/history-of-interior-design.html. Retrieved February 7, 2016.

Kelly, R. (1989). Keynote address presented at the Graphic Design Education Association Conference, Chicago IL, June 23, 1989. "The Early Years of Graphic Design at Yale University." *Design Issues.* Volume 17, Number 3, Summer 2001. pp. 3–14.

Krippendorff, K. (2006). *The Semantic Turn: A New Foundation for Design.* New York, NY: Taylor and Francis.

Leiss, W. et al. (1990). *Social Communication in Advertising.* London: Routledge.

Library of Congress. *Rise of Industrial America 1876–1900: Immigration to the United States 1851–1900.* http://www.loc.gov/teachers/classroommaterials/presentations andactivities/presentations/timeline/riseind/immgnts/. Retrieved February 16, 2016.

Lindinger, H. (1991). *Ulm Design: The Morality of Objects.* Cambridge, MA: MIT Press.

Loeffler, J. C. (2002). "Recovered Memory." *Harvard Magazine*, September–October, 2002. http://harvardmagazine.com/2002/09/recovered-memory.html.

McCoy, K. (1990). "The New Discourse." *Cranbrook Design: The New Discourse.* New York, NY: Rizzoli.

Müller, J. and Spitz, R. (2014). *HfG Ulm: A Brief History of the Ulm School of Design.* Zurich, Switzerland: Lars Müller Publishers.

Norman, D. and Stappers, P. J. (2016). "Design X: Design and Complex Sociotechnical Systems" *She-Ji: The Journal of Design, Economics, and Innovation.* Shanghai: Tongji University. p. 1.

Puetz, A. (1999). "Design Instruction for Artisans in Eighteenth-Century Britain." *Journal of Design History.* Volume 12, Number 3. Eighteenth-Century Markets and Manufactures in England and France. pp. 217–239.

Read, G. (2005). Reviewed works: "The Struggle for Modernism: Architecture, Landscape Architecture, and City Planning at Harvard." *Journal of the Society of Architectural Historians.* Volume 64, Number 1, March 2005. Berkeley, CA: University of California Press. pp. 116–118.

Rittel, H. and Webber, M. (1973). "Dilemmas in a General Theory of Planning." *Policy Sciences 4.* Amsterdam, NL: Elsevier Scientific Publishing Company. pp. 155–169.

Robinson, R. (2016). Interview conducted by Meredith Davis on January 6, 2016.

Rock, M. (1996). "Introduction." *AIGA Journal.* Volume 13, Number 1.

Salama, A. (1995). *New Trends in Architectural Education: Designing the Design Studio.* Raleigh, NC: Tailored Text and Unlimited Potential Publishing.

Stapley, M. (1911). "Thomas Jefferson: The Architect." *Architectural Record.* Volume 29, January–June, 1911. New York, NY: Architectural Record Co.

Venturi, R. (1966). *Complexity and Contradiction in Architecture.* New York, NY: Museum of Modern Art.

Weisner-Hanks, M., Wheeler, W., and Curtis, K. (2003). "Craft Guilds: Economic Change and Social Conflict." *Discovering the Medieval Past.* Boston, MA: Cengage Publishing. pp. 225–239.

Wild, L. (1994). "On Overcoming Modernism." Reprinted from *ID Magazine*, September/October 1992, in *Looking Closer: Critical Writings on Graphic Design.* Bierut, Drenteel, Heller, and Holland, eds. New York, NY: Allworth Press.

Wild, L. and Sandhaus, L. (2000). "Reputations: Lorraine Wild." *Eye* magazine. Volume 9, Number 36, Summer 2000. Retrieved from http://www.eyemagazine.com/feature/article/reputations-lorraine-wild.

Wingler, H. (1969). *Bauhaus: Weimar, Dessau, Berlin, Chicago.* Cambridge, MA: MIT Press.

Winkler, D. (1997). "Design Practice and Education: Moving Beyond the Bauhaus Model." *User-Centered Graphic Design: Mass Communications and Social Change.* Frascara, J. ed. London: Taylor and Francis. pp. 129–135.

CHAPTER 2

Davis, M. (2016). "'Normal Science' and the Changing Practices of Design and Design Education." *Visible Language.* Volume 50, Number 1.

Hazelkorn, E. (2015). *Rankings and the Reshaping of Higher Education: The Battle for World-Class Excellence.* London: Palgrave MacMillan.

Kuhn, T. (1970). *The Structure of Scientific Revolutions* (second edition). Chicago: University of Chicago Press.

Lave, J. and Wenger, E. (1991). *Situated Learning: Legitimate Peripheral Participation.* Cambridge: Cambridge University Press.

NC State University. (2011). *Comprehensiveness and Interdisciplinarity.* Retrieved from the web on July 7 at: https://info.ncsu.edu/strategic-planning/wp-content/uploads/2015/11/comprehensiveness-and-interdisciplinarity-wp-fin.pdf.

Wiggins, G. and McTighe, J. (1998). *Understanding by Design.* Alexandria, VA: Association for Supervision and Curriculum Development.

CHAPTER 3

Alexander, C. (1964). *Notes on the Synthesis of Form.* Cambridge, MA: Harvard College.

Anthony, K. (1991). *Design Juries on Trial: The Renaissance of the Design Studio.* New York, NY: Van Nostrand Reinhold.

Davis, M. (2016). "Normal Science and the Changing Practices of Design and Design Education." *Visible Language.* Number 50, Issue 1.

Dubberly, H. and Evenson, S. (2010). "Designing for Service: Creating an Experience Advantage." *Introduction to Service Engineering.* Hoboken, NJ: John Wiley and Sons, Inc.

Gans, H. (1974). *Popular Culture and High Culture: An Analysis and Evaluation of Taste.* New York, NY: Basic Books, Inc.

Lave, J. and Wenger, E. (1991). *Situated Learning: Legitimate Peripheral Participation.* Cambridge: Cambridge University Press.

Shulman, L. S. (2005) "Signature Pedagogies in the Profession." *Daedalus.* Summer 2005.

Wiggins, G. and McTighe, J. (2013). *Essential Questions: Opening Doors to Student Understanding.* Alexandria, VA: Association for Supervision and Curriculum Development.

CHAPTER 4

AIGA/NASAD. (2002). *Developing Curricula for Experience Design.* New York, NY: AIGA and NASAD.

Bialik, C. (2010). "Seven Careers in a Lifetime? Think Again, Researchers Say." *Wall Street Journal.* September 4, 2010. Retrieved on June 4, 2016 from: http://www.wsj.com/articles/SB10001424052748704206804575468162805877990.

Boyer, E. (1981). *Common Learning: A Carnegie Colloquium on General Education.* Washington, DC: Carnegie Foundation for the Advancement of Teaching. Retrieved on July 11 from: https://archive.org/stream/ERIC_ED276329/ERIC_ED276329_djvu.txt.

Davis, M. et al. (2002). *NASAD/AIGA Briefing Paper on General Education and Professional Graphic Design Curricula.* New York, NY: AIGA and NASAD.

Davis, M. (2012). "Leveraging Graduate Education for a More Relevant Future." *Envisioning a Future Design Education.* Poggenpohl, S., ed. Providence, RI: Visible Language and Rhode Island School of Design.

Davis, M. (2015). "Interdisciplinarity and the Education of the Design Generalist." *The Education of a Graphic Designer* (third edition). Steven Heller, ed. New York, NY: Allworth Press.

Elkins, J. (2003). *Visual Studies: A Skeptical Introduction.* New York, NY: Routledge.

Klein, J. T. (1990). *Interdisciplinarity: History, Theory, and Practice.* Detroit, MI: Wayne State University Press.

Malone, E. (2002). "AIGA Experience Design—Past, Present, and Future." Retrieved on June 6, 2016 from: http://boxesandarrows.com/aiga-experience-design-past -present-and-future/.

Manfra, L. (2005). "Research—Its Role in North American Design Education." *Metropolis.* http://www. metropolismag. com/PDF_files/SchoolSurvey2005.pdf.

Menand, L. (2010). *The Marketplace of Ideas: Reform and Resistance in the American University.* New York, NY: W. W. Norton & Company.

Robinson, R. E. (2016). Interview conducted by Meredith Davis on January 6, 2016 for an article for *Visible Language.*

CHAPTER 5

Anthony, K. (1991). *Design Juries on Trial: The Renaissance of the Design Studio.* New York, NY: Van Nostrand Reinhold.

Cross, N. (2006). *Designerly Ways of Knowing.* London: Springer.

Csikszentmihalyi, M. (1996). *Creativity: Flow and the Psychology of Discovery and Invention.* New York, NY: Harper Collins Publishers.

Dewey, J. (1910). *How We Think.* Lexington, MA: Heath Publishing.

Facione, P. (2010). "Critical Thinking: What It Is and Why It Counts." Retrieved from http://www.insightassessment.com/dex.html. pp. 3.1–3.18.

Halpern, D. (2003). *Thought and Knowledge: Introduction to Critical Thinking* (fourth edition). Mahwah, NJ: Lawrence Erlbaum Associates, Publishers.

Jackson, P. (1983). "The Daily Grind . . ." in *The Hidden Curriculum and Moral Education: Deception or Discovery?* Giroux, H. and Purpel, D. eds. Berkeley, CA: McCutchan. pp. 28–60.

King, P. and Kitchener, K. (1994). *Developing Reflective Judgment: Understanding and Promoting Intellectual Growth and Critical Thinking in Adolescents and Adults.* San Francisco, CA: Jossey-Bass Publishers.

Light, R. (1990). "The Harvard Assessment Seminars." *Strengthening Colleges and Universities.* Retrieved on March 8, 2016 from https://net.educause.edu/ir/library/ pdf/ffp0604.pdf.

Rojstaczer, S. (2016). Grade Inflation. Retrieved on June 6, 2016 from: http://www.
    gradeinflation.com.
Rosenman, M. and Gero, J. (1993) "Creativity in Design Using a Design Prototype
    Approach." In Gero and Maher, eds. *Modeling Creativity and Knowledge-Based
    Creative Design.* Hillsdale, NJ: Lawrence Erlbaum. pp. 106–126.
Sternberg, R. and Lubart, T. (1999). "Concepts of Creativity: Prospects and Para-
    digms." *Handbook of Creativity.* New York, NY: Cambridge University Press.
Wiggins, G. and McTighe, J. (2005). *Understanding by Design.* Alexandria, VA: Associa-
    tion for Supervision and Curriculum Development.

CHAPTER 6

Avvisati, F., Jacotin, G., and Vincent-Lancrin, S. (2013). "Educating Higher Education
    Students for Innovative Economies: What International Data Tell Us." *Tuning
    Journal for Higher Education.* Issue No. 1, November 2013. pp. 223–240.
American Association for the Advancement of Science, Project 2061. (1993). *Bench-
    marks for Science Literacy.* New York, NY: Oxford University Press.
Center for Civic Education. (1994). *National Standards for Civics and Government.*
    Calabasas, CA: Center for Civic Education.
Consortium of National Art Education Associations. (1994). *National Standards for Art
    Education: What Every Young American Should Know and Be Able to Do in the Arts.*
    Reston, VA: Music Educators National Conference.
Cross, N. (2006). *Designerly Ways of Knowing.* London: Springer.
Cuseo, J. (2007). "The Empirical Case against Large Class Size: Adverse Effects on
    the Teaching, Learning, and Retention of First-Year Students." *Journal of Faculty
    Development.* Volume 21, Number 1. Stillwater, OK: New Forums Press. pp. 5–21.
Davis, Meredith, Hawley, P., and Spilka, G. (1997). *Design as a Catalyst for Learning.*
    Alexandria, VA: Association for Supervision and Curriculum Development.
Davis, M. et al. (1998). *Design as a Catalyst for Learning.* Alexandria, VA: Association for
    Supervision and Curriculum Development.
Davis, M. and Littlejohn, D. (2016). "The Culture of Practice: Design-Based Teaching
    and Learning." *Taking Design Thinking to School.* Goldman, S., ed. London: Rout-
    ledge.
Florida, R. (2005). "The World Is Spiky." *The Atlantic Monthly.* October 2005. Wash-
    ington, DC: Atlantic Media. pp. 48–51.
Geography Education Standards Project. (1994). *Geography for Life: National Geography
    Standards.* Washington, DC: National Geographic Research and Exploration.
Gibb, N. (Minister of State for Schools). (2015). "Education Reform: Revised Design
    and Technology GCSE Content." Written statement HCWS290, November 4,
    2015. Retrieved on July 1, 2016 from: https://www.parliament.uk/business/pub-
    lications/written-questions-answers-statements/written-statement/Commons
    /2015-11-04/HCWS290/.

IDEO. (2016). *Design Thinking for Educators Toolkit*. https://www.ideo.com/work/toolkit-for-educators.

Kimbell, R. et al. (1991). *The Assessment of Performance in Design and Technology*. London: School Examinations and Assessment Council.

King, P. and Kitchener, K. (1994). *Developing Reflective Judgment: Understanding and Promoting Intellectual Growth and Critical Thinking in Adolescents and Adults*. San Francisco, CA: Jossey-Bass Publishers.

Martin, R. (2009). *Ontario in the Creative Age*. Toronto, Ontario: The Prosperity Institute.

National Center for Educational Statistics. (2016). *National Assessment of Educational Progress in Technology and Engineering Literacy*. https://nces.ed.gov/nationsreportcard/tel/moreabout.aspx.

National Council of Teachers of English and International Reading Association. (1996). *Standards for English Language Arts*. Urbana, IL and Newark, DE: National Council of Teachers of English and International Reading Association.

NC State University. (2014). *Quality Enhancement Plan: Higher Order Skills in Critical and Creative Thinking*. Raleigh, NC: NC State University.

OECD. (2015). *The Innovation Imperative: Contributing to Productivity, Growth, and Well-Being*. Paris, France: OECD.

Schön, D. (1983). *The Reflective Practitioner: How Professionals Think in Action*. New York, NY: Basic Books.

Simon, H. (1996). *The Sciences of the Artificial* (third edition). Cambridge, MA: MIT Press.

Spear, K. ed. (1984). *Rejuvenating Introductory Courses*. San Francisco, CA: Jossey-Bass Publishers.

Wilson, B. (1997). *The Quiet Evolution: Change the Face of Arts Education*. Los Angeles, CA: Getty Education Institute for the Arts.

CHAPTER 7

Common Core State Standards Initiative. (2016). *English Language Arts Standards: Writing*. Retrieved on July 31, 2016 from http://www.corestandards.org/ELA-Literacy/W/7/3/a/ and from http://www.corestandards.org/ELA-Literacy/RL/3/3/.

Gordon, W. J. J. (1973). *The Metaphorical Way of Learning and Knowing: Applying Synectics to Sensitivity and Learning Situations*. Cambridge. MA: Porpoise Books.

Knowledgeworks Foundation. (2008). *2020 Forecast: Creating the Future of Learning*. Cincinnati, OH: Knowledgeworks Foundation. Retrieved February 7, 2016 from http://www. knowledgeworks.org/sites/default/files/2020-Forecast.pdf.

Mandler, J. (1984, 2009). *Stories, Scripts, and Scenes: Aspects of Schema Theory*. New York, NY: Psychology Press, Taylor and Francis Group.

McKim, R. (1972). *Experiences in Visual Thinking*. Monterey, CA: Brooks/Cole Publishing Company.

National Assessment Governing Board. (2014). *Technology and Engineering Literacy Framework*. Retrieved June 30, 2016 from https://www.nagb.org/content/

nagb/assets/documents/publications/frameworks/technology/2014-technology-framework-abridged.pdf.

National History Education Clearinghouse. (2016). *Connecticut Standards.* Retrieved on July 22, 2016 from: http://teachinghistory.org/teaching-materials/state-standards/connecticut/1.

National Research Council and National Academy of Sciences. (1996). National Science Education Standards. Washington, DC: National Academy Press.

NYC Department of Education. (2015). *K-8 Social Studies Scope & Sequence.* New York, NY: NYC Department of Education. Retrieved on July 30, 2016 from http://schools.nyc.gov/NR/rdonlyres/82AC428B-068D-4DE1-95C2-8F7192B6D563/0/scopeandsequenceK8topbindingweb.pdf.

Next Generation Science Standards. (2013). *Science and Engineering Practices: Developing and Using Models.* Next Generation Science Standards and National Science Teachers Association. Retrieved on June 30, 2016 from http://ngss.nsta.org/Practices.aspx?id=2.

Norman, D. (1993). *Things That Make Us Smart: Defending Human Attributes in the Age of the Machine.* Reading, MA: Addison-Wesley Publishing.

North Carolina Department of Public Instruction. (2013). *Instructional Support Tools for Achieving New Standards.* Raleigh, NC: Department of Public Instruction. Retrieved on August 1, 2016 from http://www.dpi.state.nc.us/docs/curriculum/socialstudies/.

South Carolina Department of Education. (2007). *Science Standards Support Document.* Retrieved on August 18, 2016 from https://ed.sc.gov/scdoe/assets/file/agency/ccr/Standards-Learning/documents/3–2ScienceSupportDocument.pdf.

Wurman, R. (1990). *Information Anxiety: What to Do When Information Doesn't Tell You What You Need to Know.* New York, NY: Bantam.

INDEX

 **Books from Allworth Press**

Business and Legal Forms for Graphic Designers, Fourth Edition
by *Tad Crawford and Eva Doman Bruck* (8 ½ x 11, 256 pages, paperback, $29.95)

Design Literacy, Second Edition
by *Steven Heller* (6 x 9, 304 pages, paperback, $22.50)

Designers Don't Read
by *Austin Howe* (5 ½ x 8 ¼, 224 pages, paperback, $19.95)

Education of a Graphic Designer, Third Edition
by *Steven Heller* (6 x 9, 380 pages, paperback, $19.99)

The Elements of Graphic Design, Second Edition
by *Alex W. White* (8 x 10, 224 pages, paperback, $29.95)

Graphic Design Rants and Raves
by *Steven Heller* (7 x 9, 200 pages, paperback, $19.99)

How to Think Like a Great Graphic Designer
by *Debbie Millman* (6 x 9, 248 pages, paperback, $24.95)

Listening to Type
by *Alex W. White* (8 x 10, 272 pages, paperback, $29.99)

Looking Closer 5
by *Michael Beirut, William Drenttel, and Steven Heller* (6 ¼ x 9 ¼, 256 pages, paperback, $21.95)

Starting Your Career as a Graphic Designer
by *Michael Fleishman* (6 x 9, 384 pages, paperback, $19.95)

Teaching Graphic Design, Second Edition
by *Steven Heller* (6 x 9, 304 pages, paperback, $24.99)

To see our complete catalog or to order online, please visit
www.allworth.com.